Mastering Microsoft Dynamics 365 Business Central

A Comprehensive Guide to Successful Implementation

Dr. Gomathi S

Apress®

Mastering Microsoft Dynamics 365 Business Central: A Comprehensive Guide to Successful Implementation

Dr. Gomathi S
Coimbatore, Tamil Nadu, India

ISBN-13 (pbk): 979-8-8688-0229-4   ISBN-13 (electronic): 979-8-8688-0230-0
https://doi.org/10.1007/979-8-8688-0230-0

Managing Director, Apress Media LLC: Welmoed Spahr
Acquisitions Editor: Smriti Srivastava
Development Editor: Laura Berendson
Coordinating Editor: Jessica Vakili

Cover designed by eStudioCalamar

Cover image by Freepik.com

Distributed to the book trade worldwide by Apress Media, LLC, 1 New York Plaza, New York, NY 10004, U.S.A. Phone 1-800-SPRINGER, fax (201) 348-4505, e-mail orders-ny@springer-sbm.com, or visit www.springeronline.com. Apress Media, LLC is a California LLC and the sole member (owner) is Springer Science + Business Media Finance Inc (SSBM Finance Inc). SSBM Finance Inc is a **Delaware** corporation.

For information on translations, please e-mail booktranslations@springernature.com; for reprint, paperback, or audio rights, please e-mail bookpermissions@springernature.com.

Apress titles may be purchased in bulk for academic, corporate, or promotional use. eBook versions and licenses are also available for most titles. For more information, reference our Print and eBook Bulk Sales web page at http://www.apress.com/bulk-sales.

Any source code or other supplementary material referenced by the author in this book is available to readers on GitHub (https://github.com/Apress). For more detailed information, please visit https://www.apress.com/gp/services/source-code.

Paper in this product is recyclable

In loving memory of my mother, Janaki, whose spirit and love continue to guide me.

To my father, Srinivasan, for his enduring support and wisdom, and to my husband, Anantha Krishnan, for his unwavering belief in me and endless encouragement.

This book is a reflection of the strength and inspiration you have all brought into my life.

Table of Contents

About the Author

Dr. Gomathi S is a Microsoft Most Valuable Professional (MVP) and a Microsoft Certified Trainer (MCT), renowned for her expertise in data analytics and machine learning Power Platforms. She holds multiple certifications, including Microsoft Certified Data Analyst Associate and Power Platform Solution Architect Expert, and Microsoft Power App Maker Associate.

With over 13 years of experience in academia and industry, Dr. Gomathi has distinguished herself as a skilled trainer and professor, specializing in Power App, Power BI, Business Central, data science, ETL tools, and machine learning.

Her accolades include several Asia Books of Record, India Books of Record, and "Young Scientist" and "Women Scientist" awards, highlighting her contributions to the field of research and data analytics.

As a holder of six national and international patents, she continues to inspire and lead in the ever-evolving world of technology and analytics.

Acknowledgments

This book, a culmination of my dreams and efforts, would not have been possible without the support and love of several incredible individuals.

Firstly, I extend my heartfelt gratitude to my family—Lakshmi, Appadurai, Viswanathan, Anantha kalyani, Gomathy, Mahalakshmi, and Padmanaban. Your constant support, encouragement, and belief in my abilities have been the backbone of my journey. Each of you has played a pivotal role in turning my dream into reality.

A special acknowledgment goes to my mentor, Srividhya, Vice President of Atna Technologies, and Gopalakrishnan, CEO of Atna Technologies. Your guidance has been invaluable to me. Your insights, wisdom, and leadership have not only shaped me but also my personal and professional growth.

To my dear friends, Indira, Kirthika, and Dhivya Prabha—thank you for being my pillars of strength. Your unwavering support and encouragement have been instrumental in my writing process. Your friendship means the world to me.

I extend my heartfelt appreciation to Smriti Srivastava (Senior Editor), Nirmal, and all the editors and publishers involved for their expertise and commitment to bringing this book to life. Their meticulous attention to detail and dedication have been instrumental in shaping this work.

I would also like to acknowledge Atna Technologies India Pvt Ltd, Microsoft, for their support and resources that have been vital in the research and writing of this book.

ACKNOWLEDGMENTS

Finally, to my readers—thank you for embarking on this journey with me. Your interest and support mean the world to me, and I hope this book resonates with you in some way.

Lastly, to you, the readers, for embarking on this journey with me. Your interest and engagement are what bring these pages to life.

With deepest gratitude,

Dr. Gomathi S

Introduction

Mastering Microsoft Dynamics 365 Business Central: A Comprehensive Guide to Successful Implementation is a meticulously crafted resource for businesses embarking on the journey of implementing Microsoft's Business Central. This book is more than just a guide; it's a comprehensive toolkit designed to navigate the complexities of enterprise resource planning (ERP) implementation.

The core of the book is structured into 14 in-depth chapters, each dedicated to a pivotal aspect of the implementation process—from understanding Business Central's capabilities and the roles of consultants to post-implementation support and future trends in ERP technology.

What sets this book apart are the carefully curated appendixes and comparison tables included. These resources serve as invaluable references for readers.

Appendixes: These sections contain supplemental materials such as checklists, templates, and detailed guidelines. They provide practical support to businesses in various stages of implementation, ensuring that nothing is overlooked. For example, an appendix might include a checklist for pre-implementation planning or a template for vendor evaluation.

Comparison Tables: These tables offer a visual and comparative analysis of different aspects of Business Central implementation. They could compare project management methodologies like Agile and Waterfall, outline different data migration strategies, or present a side-by-side evaluation of customization options. These tables are designed to aid decision-making by clearly laying out options and their respective advantages and disadvantages.

Together, these elements transform the book into a dynamic resource, bridging the gap between theory and practice. Whether you're a business leader, a technical or functional consultant, or an IT professional, *Mastering Microsoft Dynamics 365 Business Central* offers a wealth of knowledge, practical tools, and strategic insights to guide you through a successful Business Central implementation.

By the end of this book, you'll not only have a thorough understanding of the essentials of Business Central implementation but also have hands-on tools and comparative insights that will empower you to make informed decisions tailored to your business's unique needs and objectives. This book is a roadmap to not just implementing an ERP solution, but mastering it for transformative business impact.

CHAPTER 1

Introduction to Microsoft Dynamics 365 Business Central

Effective and scalable solutions are critical for organizations to manage their operations in the fast-paced, fiercely competitive business world of today. A popular option that provides a thorough and integrated approach to business administration is Microsoft Dynamics 365 Business Central. Business Central is a cloud-based enterprise resource planning (ERP) system that has become quite popular because of its capacity to optimize and streamline a number of business functions.

Fundamentally, Microsoft Dynamics 365 Business Central acts as a centralized platform that integrates key business processes, facilitating easy departmental collaboration and data sharing. Its cloud-based architecture, which enables organizations to access their data and apps from any location at any time on any device, is one of its biggest benefits. As a result, businesses are more equipped to adapt quickly to shifting consumer needs, market conditions, and industry trends.

Business Central's main features as in Figure 1-1 cover a variety of business management domains, with a strong emphasis on supply chain management, limited customer relationship management (CRM), and financial management. Features like accounting, budgeting, cash flow management, and financial reporting are examples of financial

© Dr. Gomathi S 2024
Dr. Gomathi S, *Mastering Microsoft Dynamics 365 Business Central*,
https://doi.org/10.1007/979-8-8688-0230-0_1

management skills that offer real-time insights into the performance and health of the company's finances.

Figure 1-1. *Overview of Business Central*

Business Central supports supply chain optimization by streamlining procurement, inventory, and warehouse management. This leads to more seamless and productive operations at the lowest possible cost and with the highest possible profit. It facilitates improved inventory control, order tracking, and efficient supplier management for businesses.

Additionally, by strengthening client interactions, organizations can improve sales and service procedures with the help of Business Central's CRM features. Through the centralization of client data and interactions, teams are better equipped to offer prompt, individualized support, which in turn increases customer happiness and loyalty.

Apart from its fundamental features, Business Central has a wide range of connectors with various Microsoft products, including Office 365, Power BI, and Power Apps, facilitating improved data analysis and collaboration. The smooth connection with these tools makes data-driven decision-making possible and boosts productivity even more.

Business Central's scalability is another significant aspect that makes it appropriate for both larger organizations and small- and medium-sized enterprises (SMEs). Because of its flexibility, organizations may start with the modules they require and build the system as their needs change, making it an affordable and long-lasting solution.

Leading cloud-based ERP system Microsoft Dynamics 365 Business Central provides businesses with a unified and adaptable platform to efficiently manage their financial, supply chain, and customer-related operations. Its scalability and smooth connection with other Microsoft tools make it an effective option for companies looking to stay competitive, make data-driven decisions, and adjust to constantly shifting market conditions.

Key Features of Business Central

Let's examine some of the main characteristics that make Business Central an effective tool for contemporary organizations before getting into the deployment process.

Financial Management

Financial management in Business Central encompasses a comprehensive suite of robust tools and features that facilitate the effective management of an organization's financial operations. The software encompasses several functionalities, including but not limited to general ledger, accounts receivable, accounts payable, cash flow forecasting, and budgeting.

Why is it used? Financial management plays a crucial role in the effective operation of enterprises by ensuring the maintenance of precise and current financial records, the monitoring of transactions, and the oversight of cash flow. By utilizing real-time financial analytics, organizations are able to make well-informed decisions pertaining to the allocation of budgets, management of expenses, and formulation of investment strategies. The utilization of financial control aids firms in the maintenance of their financial operations, adherence to established accounting standards, and the preservation of their financial stability.

Example: By utilizing the financial management capabilities of Business Central, a company could effectively monitor and record its income and expenses by means of the general ledger. This software possesses the capability to generate invoices and effectively handle accounts receivable, hence facilitating the monitoring and management of outstanding payments. Through the process of cash flow forecasting, organizations can strategically allocate resources and make informed decisions regarding expenditures and investments, so assuring sufficient financial provisions to meet operational requirements and facilitate corporate expansion.

Supply Chain Management

What is it? Supply chain administration in Business Central encompasses a range of tools and features that facilitate the effective administration of inventories, order processing, and purchase planning.

Why is it used? Efficient supply chain management plays a pivotal role in enabling organizations to fulfill client requirements, optimize inventory levels, minimize lead times, and enhance overall operational efficacy. The supply chain management tools offered by Business Central assist firms in mitigating the risks of stockouts or overstock situations, reducing carrying costs, and facilitating a smooth and uninterrupted movement of goods and services from suppliers to customers.

Example: By leveraging the supply chain management capabilities of Business Central, a retail organization may effectively oversee and control its inventory levels, streamline the processing of customer orders, and strategically plan procurement activities in accordance with demand projections. Through the optimization of its supply chain, the company may effectively reduce storage expenses and enhance delivery deadlines for clients, hence resulting in heightened levels of customer happiness and loyalty.

Sales and Marketing

What is it? The Sales and Marketing features inside the Business Central system encompass the management of sales leads, the tracking of prospects, and the efficient handling of client interactions.

Why is it used? The incorporation of sales and marketing features is crucial for firms in order to cultivate potential clients, turn prospects into paying customers, and uphold robust customer connections. The capabilities provided by Business Central in this domain facilitate the optimization of sales processes, monitoring of customer interactions, and effective management of marketing campaigns. These functionalities collectively contribute to the augmentation of sales growth and the improvement of customer satisfaction.

Example: By utilizing the sales and marketing functionalities of Business Central, a software company may effectively oversee its sales leads, monitor interactions with prospective customers, and evaluate consumer preferences. This enables the sales staff to customize their approach, offer individualized solutions, and enhance their effectiveness in closing business.

Project Cost Management

What is it? The Project Management features offered by Business Central encompass a range of tools that enable firms engaged in project-based operations to effectively monitor project progress, allocate resources, and track project expenditures.

Why is it used? The incorporation of project management elements facilitates the maintenance of organizational structure inside organizations, ensuring the timely and cost-effective completion of projects, as well as the optimal utilization of available resources. This software enables project managers to monitor project milestones, effectively manage project budgets, and efficiently allocate resources, resulting in favorable project outcomes.

Example: The utilization of Business Central's project management tools by an engineering business enables the monitoring of project expenses, allocation of engineers to designated tasks, and real-time tracking of project progress. This facilitates the organization in successfully completing projects within the designated timeframe and allocated resources, leading to enhanced client contentment and the potential for recurring business opportunities.

Business Intelligence and Reporting

What is it? The Business Central platform offers a comprehensive suite of Business Intelligence and Reporting features, which include integrated tools that facilitate the creation of dynamic dashboards and configurable reports. These functionalities enable users to gain vital insights into the success of their business operations.

Why is it used? Business Intelligence (BI) and Reporting capabilities enable organizations to examine essential performance metrics, detect patterns, and formulate decisions based on data. The utilization of this technology allows individuals to acquire a more profound comprehension of their business activities, overall performance, and areas that require enhancement. Consequently, this leads to enhanced strategic planning and operational effectiveness.

Example: By utilizing the business intelligence capabilities of Business Central, a retail chain has the ability to generate interactive dashboards for the purpose of monitoring sales patterns, tracking inventory turnover rates, and identifying the stores that exhibit the highest levels of performance. The utilization of a data-driven strategy facilitates the optimization of inventory management, the identification of growth prospects, and the making of informed expansion decisions by the organization.

Integration with Microsoft 365

What is it? The integration of Microsoft 365 entails the smooth communication between Business Central and other Microsoft programs, including Microsoft Outlook and Microsoft Excel.

Why is it used? The integration of Microsoft 365 promotes productivity and cooperation by providing users with the ability to access Business Central data and carry out tasks within the familiar Microsoft applications. This feature obviates the necessity of toggling between various software applications and streamlines day-to-day operational processes.

Example: The link between Business Central and Microsoft 365 enables the HR department to conveniently retrieve personnel data from Business Central through the Microsoft Outlook platform. The integration of various HR operations, such as leave request management and employee information updates, enhances the efficiency of the HR staff and diminishes administrative burdens.

Customization and Extension

What is it? Customization and extension within the context of company Central pertain to the capacity to adapt and enhance the system in accordance with particular company needs. This entails the inclusion of personalized fields, the development of distinct workflows, and the incorporation of third-party apps.

Why is it used? Customization and extension are crucial because every business has unique processes and needs. By tailoring Business Central to their specific requirements, organizations can optimize their operations, improve efficiency, and enhance decision-making.

Examples:

- **Custom Fields**: A manufacturing company can add custom fields to track specialized production metrics that are unique to its industry.

- **Workflow Automation**: A service-based business can create workflows which are highly configurable. For instance, consider a scenario in the education sector. A school can set up a custom workflow to automate the approval process for petty cash requests. This eliminates the need for manual tasks, such as paper-based approvals, streamlining the financial processes in an educational institution.

- **Integration**: An e-commerce business can integrate Business Central with an external e-commerce platform to streamline order processing and inventory management.

Security and Compliance

What it is: Security and compliance features in Business Central are designed to safeguard sensitive data and ensure that the system adheres to industry regulations and standards. This includes user access controls, data encryption, audit trails, and compliance with data protection laws.

Why it is used: Security and compliance are essential to protect the confidentiality, integrity, and availability of business data. It helps businesses maintain trust with customers, partners, and regulatory bodies while minimizing the risk of data breaches and legal issues.

Examples:

- **Role-Based Security**: Business Central allows administrators to define user roles and permissions, ensuring that users have access only to the data and functionality necessary for their roles.

- **Data Encryption**: Sensitive data, such as financial information, can be encrypted to prevent unauthorized access in case of a security breach.

- **Audit Trails:** The system can record user activities and changes to data, providing a clear audit trail for compliance purposes.

- **GDPR Compliance**: Business Central is equipped with features that facilitate compliance with the General Data Protection Regulation (GDPR). These features assist organizations in effectively managing and safeguarding personal data in accordance with the requirements outlined in GDPR.

- **Azure AD and AD for User Authentication**: Business Central enhances its security measures by integrating with Azure Active Directory (Azure AD) and Active Directory (AD). This integration fortifies the user authentication processes within the system, providing an additional layer of security to protect sensitive data and user access in Business Central.

Scalability

What it is: Scalability in Business Central refers to the system's ability to accommodate the changing needs and growth of a business. It means that as a company expands, the ERP system can adapt to handle increased data, users, and complexity without major disruptions.

Why it is used: Scalability ensures that a business can continue to use the same ERP system as it grows, eliminating the need for costly migrations to larger systems. It also enables businesses to be agile and responsive to market changes.

Examples:

- **Adding Users:** A small business can start with a few users and easily scale up by adding more users to the system as it grows.

- **Expanding Product Lines:** An e-commerce business can introduce new product categories and sales channels without requiring a complete ERP system overhaul.

- **International Expansion**: As a company expands into new markets, Business Central can adapt to support multiple currencies and languages.

Multi-language and Multi-currency Support

What it is: Multi-language and multi-currency support in Business Central mean that the system is equipped to function in different languages and handle transactions involving various currencies.

Why it is used: This capability is particularly valuable for international businesses that operate across multiple regions or countries. It enables these businesses to maintain consistency in their financial reporting, invoicing, and communication processes, regardless of the languages spoken or currencies used. Localization caters to country-specific tax regulations and compliance requirements. It encompasses multi-language support, ensuring that the software adapts not only to languages but also to the specific financial and tax needs of various regions or countries.

Examples:

- **Global Sales**: An export-oriented company can use Business Central to manage sales in different countries, issuing invoices in the local currency and language.

- **Financial Reporting**: Multi-currency support ensures accurate financial reporting, even for companies with diverse international operations.

- **Supplier Management**: Businesses can efficiently manage suppliers from around the world, handling transactions in different currencies and languages as needed.

The 2023 release wave 2 for Dynamics 365 Business Central brings a host of new features and enhancements. Key areas of focus include integrating with Power Platform tools, enhancing core application functionalities for better business process optimization, and expanding AI capabilities through features like Copilot. This update also extends support for more countries and regions, alongside improvements in development, governance, administration, and user experiences. Businesses using D365 Business Central can look forward to more efficient, streamlined operations and enhanced capabilities in various sectors, from financial management to warehouse operations.

Microsoft Dynamics 365 Business Central provides an extensive range of functionalities that cater to diverse facets of contemporary business administration. Business Central is a robust solution that enables organizations to improve their operational efficiency, facilitate data-driven decision-making, and attain overall business growth. It encompasses a wide range of functionalities, including financial control, supply chain optimization, sales and marketing support, project management, business intelligence, and seamless integration with Microsoft 365.

Technical Consultant and Functional Consultant

Who Is a Business Central Technical Consultant?

A Business Central technical consultant is an expert individual who specializes in the technical facets of deploying, customizing, and sustaining Microsoft Dynamics 365 Business Central. Business Central is classified as an enterprise resource planning (ERP) solution, and within this framework, technical consultants hold a crucial position in guaranteeing the proper functionality of the software and its alignment with the distinct requirements of the organization.

The role of a Business Central technical consultant involves providing expertise and support in the implementation and extensions of Microsoft Dynamics 365 Business Central, a comprehensive business management solution. These professionals work closely with clients to understand their specific business requirements and translate them into technical solutions within the Business Central platform. They are responsible for configuring and customizing the system, conducting system testing, and providing training and support to end users. Additionally, Business Central technical consultants collaborate with other team members, such as functional consultants and developers, to ensure successful project delivery. Overall, their role is crucial in helping organizations optimize their use of Business Central and achieve their business objectives.

A Business Central technical consultant is a professional with specialized expertise in the field of Microsoft Dynamics 365 Business Central, which is a robust enterprise resource planning (ERP) solution. The major responsibility of software engineers is to manage the technical components of software in order to ensure its alignment with the specific needs and demands of an organization.

The following are essential components of the role of a Business Central technical consultant:

1. **System Configuration:** The Business Central system is configured in accordance with the business operations and requirements of the organization. This process entails the establishment of modules, the delineation of data structures, and the configuration of workflows.

2. The task of **customization** falls under the purview of technical consultants, who are entrusted with the responsibility of modifying the software to align with the specific requirements of the organization, in cases where the pre-existing capabilities do not adequately fulfill those needs. This encompasses the ability to generate personalized fields, reports, and extensions.

3. **Integration** involves the process of establishing seamless connectivity between Business Central and other systems and applications utilized inside the organization. This may entail integrating it with accounting software, e-commerce platforms, or other specialized tools.

4. The process of **data migration** is supervised by technical consultants, who are responsible for transferring data from current systems to Business Central. The implementation of this measure guarantees the preservation and accessibility of past data within the new system.

5. **Troubleshooting:** In the event of technical difficulties, these professionals intervene to identify and rectify the faults. This may entail the identification and resolution of software defects, optimization challenges, or challenges related to system integration.

6. The responsibility of **managing system upgrades** and updates is to ensure that the software remains up-to-date with the most recent features and security fixes.

7. **Documentation** plays a crucial role in IT initiatives, as it provides comprehensive and detailed information. Technical consultants are responsible for producing documentation that provides a comprehensive overview of the system's architecture, customizations, and integrations. This documentation serves the purpose of enhancing the comprehension and facilitation of system maintenance for other members of the team.

8. **Performance optimization** involves the ongoing monitoring of system performance and the implementation of adjustments aimed at enhancing speed and efficiency.

9. The provision of **training and support** is a crucial aspect of technical consultancy, as it enables end users and support teams to acquire the necessary skills and knowledge to proficiently utilize and address issues with the system.

Who Is a Business Central Functional Consultant?

A professional specializing in the functional aspects of adopting and customizing Microsoft Dynamics 365 Business Central, an enterprise resource planning (ERP) solution, is referred to as a Microsoft Dynamics 365 Business Central functional consultant. The major responsibility of ERP professionals is to comprehend the operational procedures and demands of an enterprise and thereafter customize the ERP system to align with those requirements.

A Business Central functional consultant is someone who works with clients to understand their business needs and then helps them implement and customize Microsoft Dynamics 365 Business Central, a comprehensive business management solution. They are responsible for gathering requirements, conducting workshops, and configuring the software to meet the specific needs of the client's organization. Additionally, they provide training and support to end users, ensuring a smooth transition to the new system. Overall, a Business Central functional consultant plays a crucial role in optimizing business processes and improving efficiency for organizations using Microsoft Dynamics 365 Business Central.

A Business Central functional consultant is a proficient professional who specializes in optimizing the functionality of Microsoft Dynamics 365 Business Central for organizational purposes. Their primary objective is to gain a comprehensive understanding of a company's operational processes and customize software solutions accordingly, in order to meet the specific requirements of the organization.

15

The following are essential components of the role and responsibilities of a Business Central functional consultant:

1. **Understanding Business Requirements:** The initial phase involves acquiring a comprehensive understanding of the operational intricacies of a corporate entity. The individuals engage in consultations with stakeholders, pose inquiries, and conduct an examination of procedures in order to comprehend the distinctive requirements of the organization.

2. **System Configuration:** It is the process of configuring Business Central based on the organization's specific requirements, with functional consultants utilizing their expertise in order to accomplish this task. The modules are established, workflows are defined, and settings are configured in order to ensure alignment between the system and the business processes.

3. **Security** procedures are implemented and maintained in order to safeguard the data held in Business Central. This include the establishment of user roles and permissions, the deployment of data encryption mechanisms, and the establishment of access control measures.

4. **Business Process Optimization:** Corporate process optimization is a key focus area for them, as they strive to enhance and streamline corporate processes. This may entail the optimization of workflows, the automation of tasks, and the implementation of software that facilitates streamlined and efficient operations.

5. **User Training:** It is common for functional consultants to be involved in the process of educating end users. The organization ensures that its personnel possess the necessary knowledge and skills to properly utilize the enterprise resource planning (ERP) system in order to carry out their routine responsibilities.

6. **Documentation:** It plays a key role in comprehending the intricacies of a set system. Functional consultants are responsible for generating documentation that delineates the configuration of the system, tailored procedures, and any distinctive attributes.

7. **Testing and Quality Assurance:** These individuals actively engage in the testing phase to ensure that the configured software operates accurately and aligns with the specified business requirements. All identified faults encountered during the testing phase are promptly resolved prior to the deployment of the system.

8. **Continuous Improvement:** Functional consultants do not solely execute system implementation and disengage. The performance of the system is monitored in actual business activities, and feedback is collected from users. The aforementioned data is utilized for the purpose of suggesting enhancements and modifications.

9. **Communication:** The ability to communicate effectively is crucial. Functional consultants serve as middlemen who facilitate communication and collaboration between business stakeholders and technological teams. The individuals in question possess the ability to convert the requirements of a business into technical specifications, and afterward verify that the resulting solution satisfies the expectations of both parties involved.

Table 1-1. *Difference Between Technical and Functional Consultant*

Aspect	Technical Consultant	Functional Consultant
Primary Responsibilities	Focus on the technical aspects of the software. They configure, customize, and maintain the software to meet technical requirements	Concentrate on understanding and improving business processes. They configure the software to align with the organization's business needs
Understanding of Business Processes	Understand business processes to a certain extent but primarily from a technical perspective	Deeply understand and analyze business processes and requirements
Configuration and Customization	Configure and customize the software to align with technical needs, such as integrations, data migration, and security	Configure and customize the software to align with business processes, including workflows, reports, and data structures
Integration and Data Migration	Manage integrations with other systems and handle data migration tasks as needed	Focus on integrating the software into existing business operations and ensuring data consistency

(continued)

Table 1-1. *(continued)*

Aspect	Technical Consultant	Functional Consultant
Technical Concepts to Know	– Programming languages (e.g., C/AL, AL) – Database management – Cloud infrastructure – Security protocols and measures	– Business analysis and process modeling – Workflow design – Report customization – User training and support
Documentation and Training	Document technical configurations and provide technical training to IT teams	Document business process configurations and provide end-user training for employees
Quality Assurance and Testing	Involved in technical testing, system performance, and ensuring technical aspects function correctly	Focus on functional testing and ensuring the software aligns with business requirements and processes
Communication with Stakeholders	Translate technical concepts to non-technical stakeholders and ensure alignment with business goals	Act as a bridge between technical teams and business stakeholders, translating business requirements into technical specifications
Continuous Improvement and Optimization	Monitor technical performance and recommend technical improvements	Continuously optimize and improve business processes and their alignment with the software

(continued)

Table 1-1. *(continued)*

Aspect	Technical Consultant	Functional Consultant
Security and Compliance	Typically, technical consultants primarily focus on security measures during integrations. They ensure that the system's technical aspects align with security regulations and standards. This includes handling permissions related to data access and usage	In general, functional consultants play a crucial role in configuring security settings related to user access, including permissions to view, edit, and create data. This configuration is done to meet the specific business requirements of the organization. Compliance measures, especially those related to GDPR matters, often come into play when building extensions that deal with specific regulatory needs

Tips for a Successful Business Central Implementation

The implementation of an enterprise resource preparation (ERP) system, such as Business Central, is a substantial endeavor that demands meticulous preparation and execution. In order to ensure a successful implementation, it is advisable to take into consideration the following recommendations:

1. **Establishing Clear Objectives:** Commence the process by precisely identifying the objectives associated with the implementation. What particular difficulties do you aim to tackle? What are the intended business objectives that you seek to accomplish through the utilization of Business Central? The presence of well-defined objectives serves as a guiding force throughout the entirety of the implementation process.

2. One important aspect to consider is the **involvement of key stakeholders.** It is imperative to involve essential stakeholders from many departments at the first stages of the process. The contribution of users is of utmost importance in comprehending distinct business requirements and guaranteeing that Business Central is in harmony with current operational procedures.

3. **Select the Appropriate Implementation Team:** Formulate a specialized implementation team of persons with a wide range of skills, encompassing IT specialists, departmental leaders, and end users. The team will assume the responsibility of advancing the implementation process.

4. **Data Migration Strategy:** Prior to the implementation of Business Central, it is imperative to evaluate the current data infrastructure and devise a comprehensive plan for its seamless transition to the new system. It is imperative to maintain data integrity and capitalize on the occasion to purify and amalgamate data in order to enhance its correctness.

5. **Prioritize Training and Change Management:** The prioritization of training and change management is crucial to facilitate a seamless transition to the newly implemented enterprise resource planning (ERP) system. Furthermore, it is advisable to incorporate change management tactics to effectively handle any opposition toward the newly implemented procedures and cultivate a favorable environment for their acceptance.

6. **Client-Side Considerations:** In addition to the above, consider these client-side factors for a successful implementation:

   - **Steering Committee:** Establish a steering committee responsible for overseeing the project's strategic direction.

   - **Change Management and Adoption:** Develop a robust change management and adoption strategy to ensure that employees embrace the new system.

   - **Single Point of Contact:** Designate a single point of contact to facilitate communication and issue resolution.

   - **Change Control Board:** Set up a change control board to manage changes to the project scope.

   - **Project Meetings:** Conduct regular project meetings to track progress and address issues.

- **Vendor Selection:** When selecting a vendor for
  Business Central, consider factors such as vendor staff
  certifications on D365BC, vendor experience, and
  their track record with similar implementations. The
  right vendor can significantly impact the success of
  your implementation.

By incorporating these client-side considerations and paying attention
to vendor selection, you can enhance the chances of a successful Business
Central implementation.

Business Central Application Fields

Microsoft Dynamics 365 Business Central is a versatile enterprise resource
planning (ERP) system renowned for its adaptability, making it suitable for
diverse industries and business sectors depicted in the Figure 1-2. While
Business Central offers comprehensive capabilities, it's important to note
that, out of the box, it may not provide all the specialized features required
by certain industries. However, there are two methods to address this:

> **Integration with Industry Verticals:** In cases
> where Business Central lacks certain industry-
> specific functionalities, businesses can integrate
> the system with industry-specific solutions. These
> solutions can be custom-built externally or sourced
> from Microsoft AppSource. This integration allows
> businesses to extend Business Central's capabilities
> to meet their unique industry needs.

Customization Through Extensions: Alternatively, businesses can opt to customize Business Central using extensions. This involves building specific functionalities tailored to the industry's requirements. Customizations ensure that the ERP system aligns perfectly with the demands of the industry.

Figure 1-2. Business Central Applications

Manufacturing: Business Central is a software solution that offers valuable assistance to manufacturing companies in effectively managing several aspects of their operations. These include production planning, inventory control, quality assurance, and order processing. By utilizing

Business Central, manufacturing companies may streamline these processes and enhance overall efficiency.

Supply Chain: The distribution and wholesale sector utilizes this technology to enhance order management processes, optimize inventory levels, and enhance visibility inside the supply chain.

Retail: In the retail industry, businesses employ the use of Business Central as a means to effectively oversee several aspects of their operations, including point-of-sale activities, inventory management, customer relations, and loyalty programs.

Finance and Accounting: Business Central is equipped with comprehensive financial management features, rendering it highly ideal for enterprises specializing in finance and accounting.

Here are some examples of how Business Central is applied across various industries:

Construction: Construction companies rely on Business Central to efficiently manage project lifecycles, allocate resources, and track project costs.

Education: Educational institutions utilize Business Central for financial management, student record keeping, and resource allocation.

Real Estate: Real estate enterprises use Business Central for property management, lease tracking, and financial analysis.

Government: Government bodies leverage Business Central for financial administration, procurement, and project tracking.

Pharmaceuticals: While Business Central supports various aspects of pharmaceutical business operations, it may require additional solutions or customizations to meet specific regulatory compliance requirements.

It's important to understand that while Business Central serves as a robust foundation for ERP, its full potential is realized when integrated with industry-specific solutions or customized to meet the unique demands of certain industries.

These aforementioned instances are just a glimpse of the versatility of Business Central. Together with third-party industry vertical solutions available on Microsoft AppSource, integrations with other third-party software, and the capability to customize/extend D365BC, this ERP system offers a robust and adaptable solution for a diverse array of organizations. Its inherent flexibility and scalability empower firms to tailor it precisely to their unique requirements, making it a highly valued enterprise resource planning (ERP) solution suitable for a wide range of industries and businesses.

Ideas for Implementing Business Central in Different Industries

Retailers

For retailers, Business Central has the potential to revolutionize their business by optimizing their processes and elevating client interaction. Insightful concepts for retailers include

Optimize Inventory Management: Retailers can maintain ideal stock levels, lower carrying costs, and prevent stockouts thanks to Business Central's inventory management features. Retailers may ensure that products are easily accessible for customers by making data-driven decisions about purchasing and restocking with real-time visibility into inventory levels and trends.

Automate Purchasing Processes: Retailers can streamline their procurement procedures by utilizing Business Central's purchasing automation services. By automating purchase requisitions, order creation, and vendor administration, it boosts productivity and decreases manual labor.

Establish Loyalty Programs: Retailers may use Business Central's CRM features to develop that honor devoted patrons. Retailers may create more enduring relationships with their customers and boost customer retention by providing personalized rewards and promotions based on consumer behavior and preferences.

Manufacturers

Business Central provides technologies to improve shop floor insights, production planning, and general efficiency for manufacturers. Some important implementation concepts are

Make Use of Production Planning Functions: Business Central has scheduling and production planning functions. Better resource utilization and on-time product delivery result from manufacturers'

27

ability to establish and manage production orders, track material requirements, and optimize production schedules.

Track Work Orders: Manufacturers may follow work orders from one stage of manufacturing to the next with Business Central. Through the identification of bottlenecks and the streamlining of operations, this visibility enhances production efficiency and shortens lead times.

Service-Based Businesses

Businesses that provide services can use Business Central to improve service management and obtain insightful operational data. Some important implementation concepts are

Simplify Service Management: Business Central has tools for handling resource allocation, service agreements, and service orders. These features help service-based companies plan and manage service tasks more effectively, which enhances customer happiness and service delivery.

Automate Billing Procedures: Service-based companies can use Business Central to automate the invoicing and billing procedures. This lowers billing errors and enhances cash flow management by guaranteeing timely and accurate invoicing for services performed.

Use Analytics for Service Trends: Service-based companies can analyze service data and spot trends and opportunities by utilizing Business Central's integrated business intelligence capabilities. Businesses can more successfully meet consumer needs by customizing their offers based on their understanding of client preferences and service demand patterns.

The adaptability of Microsoft Dynamics 365 Business Central makes it a flexible option for a range of sectors. Retailers can use loyalty programs to engage customers and optimize inventory. IoT integration can help manufacturers improve shop floor analytics and production planning. Businesses that provide services can use analytics to spot trends and expedite service management. Businesses may achieve operational efficiency, make data-driven choices, and obtain a competitive edge in their individual markets by customizing Business Central to meet their unique industry demands.

Summary

In this chapter, the dynamic capabilities of Microsoft Dynamics 365 Business Central have been explored. From its versatility in various industries to its adaptability through integrations and customizations, Microsoft Dynamics 365 Business Central emerges as a powerful tool for modern businesses. The ERP system's user-friendly features and robust functionalities pave the way for efficient operations, smarter decision-making, and sustainable growth. Moving forward, harnessing the full potential of Microsoft Dynamics 365 Business Central can truly transform the way organizations operate, ensuring a competitive edge in today's dynamic business landscape.

Exercises

1. Research and compile a list of companies in your industry that have successfully implemented Business Central. Analyze their case studies to understand how they achieved their objectives and overcame implementation challenges.

2. Identify the key pain points in your organization's current business processes. Brainstorm how Business Central can address these pain points and improve efficiency.

3. Form a mock implementation team with colleagues or friends. Assign roles and responsibilities, and discuss how you would approach a Business Central implementation in a fictional scenario. Document the steps you would take and the challenges you anticipate.

We will delve further into the implementation process in the following chapters, addressing a range of topics like data transfer, project management, vendor selection, testing, and more. Together, let's take on the challenge of mastering Business Central deployment and realizing all of its potential for the expansion and prosperity of your company.

CHAPTER 2

Pre-implementation Planning: Setting the Stage for Success

Overview

In the realm of Microsoft Dynamics 365 Business Central, success is born from meticulous pre-implementation planning. Before embarking on the journey of implementation, it's imperative to lay a strong foundation. This chapter is your guide, leading you through the critical steps to ensure a smooth and prosperous implementation journey.

We commence with an exploration of why pre-implementation planning is indispensable. We delve into the significance of comprehensively assessing your organization's current state, identifying pain points and challenges, and setting objectives that are specific, measurable, achievable, relevant, and time-bound (SMART). Engagement with stakeholders and practical tools for business analysis are at your disposal.

A key pillar of success is the assembly of the right implementation team. We emphasize the vital role this team plays and guide you in

© Dr. Gomathi S 2024
Dr. Gomathi S, *Mastering Microsoft Dynamics 365 Business Central*,
https://doi.org/10.1007/979-8-8688-0230-0_2

selecting individuals with the right skill sets. Representation from various departments, clear roles and responsibilities, and the introduction of a RACI matrix are highlighted. Effective communication and collaboration are underscored as essential for team synergy.

Financial prudence and a realistic timeline are the cornerstones of success. We equip you with a comprehensive budget template that covers all aspects, from software licenses to training and customization. Identifying cost-saving opportunities and allowing buffer periods for unforeseen challenges are vital considerations. Strategic resource allocation ensures that your resources are used efficiently.

In the final section, we offer you a roadmap—a visual representation of the pre-implementation journey. This roadmap serves as your compass, keeping you on course and aligned with your objectives. We stress the importance of regular reviews and adjustments to adapt to evolving business needs. It's your blueprint for a successful Business Central implementation.

This chapter provides the essential framework for effective pre-implementation planning, ensuring that you're well-prepared to embark on your journey toward implementing Microsoft Dynamics 365 Business Central. It's your guide to setting the stage for a successful and transformative experience, aligning your efforts with the objectives of your organization, and achieving efficiency, productivity, and growth.

The efficacy of a Microsoft Dynamics 365 Business Central implementation within the domain of enterprise resource planning (ERP) systems is not only contingent upon the execution phase. Rather, it is substantially derived from the careful and systematic planning and strategizing that precedes it. Welcome to Chapter 2 of our exploration, wherein we delve into the crucial stage of pre-implementation planning.

Consider the scenario of going on a cross-country road trip devoid of a navigational map, a premeditated itinerary, or any prior knowledge of the intended destination. The potential result is anticipated to be characterized by various deviations, obstacles, and interruptions. Likewise, commencing a Business Central implementation without comprehensive pre-implementation preparation might result in a comparable state of disorder and uncertainty. This chapter presents a dependable roadmap that provides guidance on the crucial stages necessary to develop a robust foundation for a successful installation of Business Central.

The Essence of Pre-implementation Planning

The foundation of a successful Microsoft Dynamics 365 Business Central implementation project lies in thorough pre-implementation planning. The process involves careful planning and strategic analysis, which can significantly impact the outcome, distinguishing between a seamless and successful execution vs a chaotic and troublesome one. The following are the fundamental components that comprise the core of pre-implementation planning:

- **Comprehensive Analysis of Current State:** The starting point of pre-implementation planning is a deep and thorough examination of your organization's current state. This involves scrutinizing existing business processes, technologies, and workflows. You need to identify what's working well, what's not, and where bottlenecks or inefficiencies exist. This analysis is the foundation upon which you'll build your future state.

- **Understanding Requirements:** During this phase, it's crucial to understand the past, present, and future challenges of your organization. These could range from outdated software systems and manual processes to data fragmentation and reporting difficulties.

33

By identifying and acknowledging these, you set the stage for targeted improvements through the Business Central implementation.

- **Defining Clear Objectives:** Pre-implementation planning also entails setting clear objectives and goals for your Business Central implementation. What do you aim to achieve with this new system? Your objectives should be specific, measurable, achievable, relevant, and time-bound (SMART). They should align with your broader organizational strategy and address the pain points identified.

- **Stakeholder Involvement:** Your stakeholders, including employees from various departments, are invaluable sources of information during this phase. Engage with them to gain insights into their specific needs and challenges. Their input can provide a holistic view of what the system should deliver and how it can improve their daily tasks.

- **Strategic Team Formation:** Another key part of pre-implementation planning involves putting together the correct implementation team. A steering committee, a change control board, an end-user team, and the project's champions from various parts of your organization should make up the team. This guarantees that the project is well-informed by your company's diverse viewpoints and requirements.

- **Clear Roles and Responsibilities:** Within the team, clearly define roles and responsibilities. A RACI (Responsible, Accountable, Consulted, Informed) matrix can help assign tasks and decision-making responsibilities. This clarity ensures that everyone knows their role in the project, reducing confusion and potential conflicts.

- **Financial Prudence:** Pre-implementation planning is the time to chart the financial course. Create a comprehensive budget that covers all costs associated with the implementation, and allocate resources wisely. Identify areas where cost-saving opportunities exist and make informed decisions about where to allocate resources for the best return on investment.

- **Realistic Timeline:** Establishing a realistic timeline is essential to managing expectations and ensuring that the project progresses as planned. This timeline should account for the scope of the project and include buffer periods to accommodate any unforeseen challenges or delays.

- **Dynamic Roadmap:** Finally, pre-implementation planning gives birth to a roadmap—a visual representation of the steps and milestones that need to be achieved. This roadmap should be dynamic and adaptable, allowing for adjustments as the planning phase evolves and as the organization's needs change.

Note   A detailed checklist for Assessing Business Needs and Requirement Gathering is provided in Appendix A.

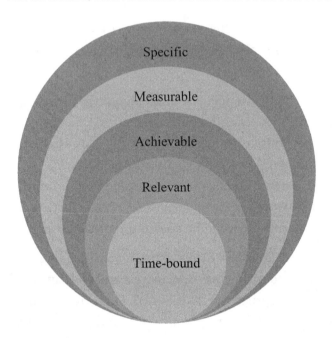

Figure 2-1. *SMART*

Accessing Business Needs and Objectives

Understanding Business Needs and Objectives

Imagine setting out on a long and ambitious journey without a clear destination in mind. The journey may be riddled with uncertainties, detours, and missed opportunities. In the world of business and technology, a Microsoft Dynamics 365 Business Central implementation is no different. It's a significant undertaking that requires meticulous planning and a profound understanding of where you are and where you aim to be.

> **Comprehensive Analysis:** The process begins with a comprehensive analysis of your organization's current state. This entails a detailed examination of your existing business processes, technology

infrastructure, and operational workflows. What's functioning efficiently, and where are the pain points that hinder productivity or growth? This analysis serves as the foundation upon which your implementation strategy will be built.

Identifying Pain Points: Within this analysis, it's vital to identify and acknowledge the pain points and challenges your organization faces. These pain points can vary widely, from outdated software systems causing inefficiencies to fragmented data leading to reporting difficulties. Recognizing these challenges is the first step toward finding solutions that will drive improvements through the Business Central implementation.

Defining SMART and Clear Objectives: In the world of navigation, a clear destination point on the map is essential. Similarly, in business, it's crucial to define clear objectives for your Business Central implementation. What do you hope to achieve with this new system? Your objectives should be specific and measurable, ensuring that you can track your progress and evaluate the success of the implementation. These objectives should also align with your organization's broader strategic goals.

SMART objectives are a crucial concept in the context of pre-implementation planning for Microsoft Dynamics 365 Business Central. SMART depicted in Figure 2-1 is an acronym that stands for specific, measurable, achievable, relevant, and time-bound. The oveLet's elaborate on what SMART objectives mean and why they are important:

Specific:

- Specific objectives are clear, concise, and unambiguous. They leave no room for interpretation or confusion. When setting specific objectives for your Business Central implementation, you should define precisely what you want to achieve. For example, instead of a vague goal like "improve efficiency," a specific objective would be "reduce order processing time by 20%."

Measurable:

- Measurable objectives are quantifiable and allow you to track progress. You should establish clear criteria or metrics to evaluate whether you've met your objectives. In the case of Business Central, this might involve measuring key performance indicators (KPIs) such as sales growth, inventory turnover, or customer satisfaction. For example, you could set an objective to "increase sales revenue by 15% within the first year of implementation."

Achievable:

- Achievable objectives are realistic and attainable within the constraints of your organization. It's essential to ensure that your objectives are within reach and can be accomplished with the available resources, budget, and expertise. Unrealistic objectives can lead to frustration and project failure. For example, setting a goal to "double revenue within a month" might not be achievable, but achieving a 10% increase in revenue might be realistic.

Relevant:

- Relevant objectives are aligned with your organization's broader goals and the purpose of the Business Central implementation. Each objective should contribute directly to improving your business processes, addressing pain points, or supporting your strategic vision. It's essential to assess whether each objective is truly relevant to the overall success of the implementation.

Time-bound:

- Time-bound objectives have a clearly defined timeframe or deadline. Setting deadlines helps create a sense of urgency and ensures that progress is monitored regularly. In Business Central implementation, time-bound objectives might involve specifying when certain milestones should be achieved. For instance, "complete user training within eight weeks of project kickoff."

Engaging Stakeholders: Your organization is a complex ecosystem with multiple departments, teams, and stakeholders. During the pre-implementation phase, it's essential to engage with these stakeholders to gain insights into their specific needs and challenges. Each department may have unique requirements that should be considered in the implementation strategy. By involving stakeholders, you ensure that the implementation is holistic and takes into account the diverse perspectives within your organization.

Tools and Templates: To facilitate this process, we provide you with practical tools and templates. These resources are designed to guide you in conducting a thorough business analysis, gathering requirements, and documenting your findings. They serve as structured frameworks that help you organize and make sense of the complex landscape of your organization's needs and objectives.

In essence, this phase of assessing business needs and objectives is akin to charting your course before setting sail. It ensures that you have a clear understanding of where you stand, where you want to go, and why you're embarking on this journey. With this knowledge firmly in hand, you can proceed to build a tailored implementation plan that addresses your organization's unique requirements and steers you toward success with Microsoft Dynamics 365 Business Central.

Forming an Implementation Team

The success of any significant undertaking, such as a Microsoft Dynamics 365 Business Central implementation, hinges significantly on the composition and capabilities of the team leading the charge. In this section, we'll explore why forming the right implementation team is paramount, how to select the right individuals for key roles, and the strategies for fostering effective communication and collaboration within the team.

The Team's Role in Success: Your implementation team is the driving force behind the project. They are the architects and builders of your Business Central solutions. Just as a well-assembled crew is essential for a ship's successful voyage, your team members play pivotal roles in steering your organization toward successful implementation.

Selecting the Right People: To form an effective implementation team, you must carefully select individuals with the right mix of skills, knowledge, and expertise. This isn't just about having IT professionals; it's about drawing representation from various departments that will be impacted by the implementation. You'll want team members from IT, finance, operations, sales, and other pertinent areas. Each department brings a unique perspective, and their input is invaluable for a holistic and effective implementation.

Defining Roles and Responsibilities: Clear roles and responsibilities within the team are essential for avoiding confusion and ensuring that tasks are executed efficiently. We introduce you to the concept of a RACI matrix—a tool that defines who is Responsible, Accountable, Consulted, and Informed for each task or decision. This matrix brings clarity to the team's dynamics, ensuring that everyone knows their role and the extent of their responsibilities.

RACI Matrix for Business Central Functional Consultant

In the world of project management and implementation, a RACI matrix is a valuable tool used to define roles and responsibilities within a team. As explained in Table 2-1, RACI Matrix for Business Central Functional Consultant, RACI stands for Responsible, Accountable, Consulted, and Informed, and it helps clarify who does what in a project. Let's break down the roles within the matrix for a Business Central Functional Consultant:

1. **Responsible (R):**

   - The "Responsible" role designates the person or role primarily responsible for performing a specific task or activity related to the implementation. In the case of a Business Central Functional Consultant:

     - The consultant is typically responsible for tasks directly related to configuring and customizing the Microsoft Dynamics 365 Business Central system. This includes setting up modules, defining workflows, and ensuring that the system aligns with the organization's business processes.

- They are accountable for the technical aspects of the system's functionality and ensuring that it meets the business requirements.

2. **Accountable (A):**

- The "Accountable" role signifies the individual or role that has ultimate ownership and decision-making authority over a particular aspect of the project. In the context of a Business Central implementation:

  - The accountable role may belong to a project manager, executive sponsor, or a high-level stakeholder who has the final say on critical decisions.

  - While the Business Central Functional Consultant has technical expertise and recommendations, the accountable role has the authority to approve or reject proposed changes, configurations, or customizations.

3. **Consulted (C):**

- The "Consulted" role involves individuals or roles that provide input, feedback, or expertise on a specific task or decision. In the Business Central implementation:

  - The consultant might need to consult with various stakeholders, such as department heads, end users, or subject matter experts within the organization.

  - They gather input and requirements from these individuals to ensure that the system aligns with the needs of different departments and teams.

4. **Informed (I):**

- The "Informed" role refers to individuals or roles that need to be kept informed about the progress of a task or decision but do not have an active role in its execution or decision-making. For a Business Central implementation:

  - Other team members, project stakeholders, or even end users may fall into the "Informed" category.

  - They receive updates on the progress of the implementation and are aware of any changes or developments.

Table 2-1. *RACI Matrix for Business Central Functional Consultant*

Aspect/Criteria	Responsible (R)	Accountable (A)	Consulted (C)	Informed (I)
Configuring Business Central	[Functional Consultant]	[Project Manager]	[Stakeholders]	[Team Members]
Customizing System	[Technical Consultant]	[Project Manager]	[Stakeholders]	[Team Members]
Gathering Requirements	[Functional Consultant]	[Project Manager]	[Stakeholders]	[Team Members]
Engaging Stakeholders	[Functional Consultant]	[Project Manager]	[Team Members]	[Executives]
Defining Clear Objectives	[Functional Consultant]	[Project Manager]	[Stakeholders]	[Team Members]
Budget Creation	[Functional Consultant]	[Project Manager]	[Finance Team]	[Stakeholders]

(*continued*)

Table 2-1. *(continued)*

Aspect/Criteria	Responsible (R)	Accountable (A)	Consulted (C)	Informed (I)
Timeline Development	[Functional and Technical Consultant]	[Project Manager]	[Team Members]	[Stakeholders]
Identifying Cost-Saving	[Functional Consultant]	[Project Manager]	[Finance Team]	[Stakeholders]
Allocating Resources	[Technical Consultant]	[Project Manager]	[Team Members]	[Finance Team]
Roadmap Development	[Technical Consultant]	[Project Manager]	[Team Members]	[Stakeholders]
Progress Tracking	[Technical and Functional Consultant]	[Project Manager]	[Team Members]	[Stakeholders]

Effective Communication and Collaboration: Effective communication and collaboration are the lifeblood of any successful implementation team. Team members must be able to share insights, provide feedback, and work together seamlessly. We emphasize the importance of fostering an environment where open communication is encouraged, and team members feel comfortable sharing their ideas and concerns. Collaboration tools and regular team meetings are instrumental in maintaining cohesion.

Dedicated Project Manager: A dedicated project manager is the linchpin of the implementation team. This individual is responsible for orchestrating the various elements of the project, managing timelines, and ensuring that everyone is aligned with the project's goals. The project manager's role is akin to the captain of a ship, steering the project toward its intended destination.

In essence, forming an effective implementation team is like building a well-balanced crew for a complex expedition. Each member brings their unique expertise, and clear roles and responsibilities are defined to avoid confusion. Effective communication and collaboration among team members are the winds that fill the project's sails, propelling it toward success. As you embark on this journey, remember that your team is not just a group of individuals; they are the architects of your organization's future with Microsoft Dynamics 365 Business Central.

Budgeting and Timeline

Embarking on a journey, whether it's a cross-country road trip or a business transformation project, demands careful financial planning and a realistic timeline. In this section, we'll explore why these aspects are crucial and provide you with guidance on creating a comprehensive budget and timeline that will set the stage for a successful Business Central implementation.

> **Financial Prudence:** Imagine setting off on a road trip without a clear budget for fuel, accommodation, and meals. Such a journey would be fraught with financial uncertainties. Similarly, your Business Central implementation requires prudent financial planning. This involves creating a comprehensive budget that encompasses all the costs associated with the project.

> **The Comprehensive Budget:** Our guide includes a comprehensive budget template that is designed to help you account for various expenses. These expenses may include software licenses, implementation services provided by consultants,

training for your team, data migration efforts, and any customizations or modifications needed to tailor Business Central to your organization's specific needs.

Identifying Cost-Saving Opportunities: Within this budgeting process, it's essential to be vigilant about identifying potential cost-saving opportunities. For instance, you can explore different options for software licensing to ensure you're getting the best value for your investment. Similarly, when it comes to implementation services, you can evaluate providers and choose the one that offers the most cost-effective solution without compromising on quality.

Realistic Timeline: Time constraints apply to every journey, no matter how well-planned. Your Business Central deployment will be no exception. A realistic timeline outlining the project's milestones, deadlines, and financial periods is critical. This timeline should take into account the project's scope as well as the numerous tasks and activities that must be completed. Aligning the chronology with your financial periods ensures that your ERP system integrates seamlessly with your financial cycles, resulting in a more synchronized and efficient overall deployment.

Buffer Periods for Unforeseen Challenges: In any significant undertaking, unexpected challenges can arise. Just as a road trip may encounter detours or delays due to road closures or inclement weather, your implementation project might face unforeseen obstacles. To mitigate these challenges, it's essential to build buffer periods into your timeline. These buffer periods allow for flexibility and the accommodation of unexpected issues without derailing the project's overall schedule.

Strategic Resource Allocation: Your budget and timeline also require strategic resource allocation. You'll need to allocate financial resources to different aspects of the project based on priority and need. For example, training and data migration may require significant investments. Additionally, you should allocate human resources to the project, ensuring that team members have the time and support they need to contribute effectively.

In summary, budgeting and timeline considerations are the financial and temporal cornerstones of your Business Central implementation. A well-structured budget ensures that you have the necessary resources to fund the project, while a realistic timeline provides a clear roadmap for the project's execution. By identifying cost-saving opportunities and incorporating buffer periods, you increase the project's chances of success while maintaining financial prudence. Ultimately, these aspects enable you to navigate the journey of Business Central implementation with confidence and foresight.

Roadmap to Success

As you embark on your journey toward implementing Microsoft Dynamics 365 Business Central, having a clear roadmap is akin to charting a course before setting sail. This roadmap serves as your guiding star, providing a visual representation of the steps and milestones that need to be achieved during the pre-implementation phase. Let's explore why a roadmap is essential and how it can contribute to the success of your project.

Visual Guidance: Think of the roadmap as your compass, a tool that offers you clear visual guidance through the complex landscape of pre-implementation planning. Just as a ship's captain relies on navigational instruments to plot a course, your roadmap provides a structured path to follow. It ensures that you remain on track and aligned with your objectives, even as the project unfolds.

Preventing Aimless Drifting: Without a roadmap, your pre-implementation planning phase could resemble aimless drifting at sea. You may find yourself unsure of which direction to take, what milestones to aim for, or when to celebrate achievements. A roadmap eliminates this ambiguity by laying out a predefined route that you can follow with confidence.

Setting Expectations: A well-constructed roadmap also serves to set expectations for everyone involved in the project. It provides a visual representation of the project's timeline and key milestones. This transparency helps stakeholders understand what to expect and when, reducing uncertainty and promoting buy-in from team members and decision-makers.

Alignment with Objectives: Every step of your roadmap is designed to keep you aligned with your organization's objectives and goals. It ensures that the tasks you undertake during the pre-implementation phase directly contribute to the success of your Business Central implementation. This alignment ensures that your efforts are purposeful and strategic.

Continuous Review and Adjustment: One of the critical features of an effective roadmap is its adaptability. Business needs can change, unforeseen challenges can arise, and new opportunities can emerge. That's why we stress the importance of continuous review and adjustment. As your business needs evolve or as new insights surface during the planning phase, your roadmap should be flexible enough to accommodate these changes. Regular reviews help ensure that the roadmap remains a relevant and effective guide.

Tracking Progress: The roadmap also serves as a tool for tracking progress. It allows you to mark off completed milestones, providing a visual representation of how far you've come. This not only offers a sense of accomplishment but also helps you evaluate whether you're on schedule and whether adjustments are needed.

In summary, a roadmap to success is more than just a visual aid—it's a strategic tool that ensures you stay on course during the pre-implementation planning phase. It keeps you aligned with your objectives, prevents aimless drifting, and provides a clear path forward.

By regularly reviewing and adjusting the roadmap as needed, you can adapt to changing circumstances and ensure that your Business Central implementation remains on track to meet your organization's goals.

This chapter summarizes the key takeaways and highlights of Chapter 2, "Pre-implementation Planning," in this book *Mastering Microsoft Dynamics 365 Business Central*.

Conclusion

In this chapter, we've embarked on the essential journey of pre-implementation planning for Microsoft Dynamics 365 Business Central. We've explored the core principles and practices that form the bedrock of a successful implementation. Let's recap the key takeaways:

1. **The Essence of Pre-implementation Planning**

    - Pre-implementation planning is the compass that guides your journey toward implementing Business Central.

    - A thorough understanding of your organization's current state, present, and future requirements and objectives is essential.

    - SMART objectives—specific, measurable, achievable, relevant, and time-bound—are the framework for success.

    - Engaging stakeholders and using practical tools for analysis are pivotal.

2. **Forming an Implementation Team**

- The right team is the engine that drives your implementation.

- A well-rounded team with representation from various departments is crucial.

- Clear roles, responsibilities, and the use of a RACI matrix ensure efficient collaboration.

- Effective communication and collaboration are fundamental for success.

3. **Budgeting and Timeline**

- Careful financial planning and realistic timelines are essential for a smooth journey.

- A comprehensive budget template covers all aspects, from licenses to training and customization.

- Identifying cost-saving opportunities and buffer periods for unforeseen challenges are critical.

- Strategic resource allocation optimizes your resources.

4. **Roadmap to Success**

- Your roadmap is the guiding star of the pre-implementation phase.

- Prevent aimless drifting by following a structured path.

- Set clear expectations and align with organizational objectives.

- Regular reviews and adjustments keep you on course.

Summary

By embracing these principles and practices, you've laid a solid foundation for your Microsoft Dynamics 365 Business Central implementation journey. Pre-implementation planning ensures that your efforts are purposeful, strategic, and aligned with your organization's goals. As you move forward, keep these insights in mind, and remember that success lies in meticulous planning and continuous adaptation.

CHAPTER 3

Vendor Selection and Partnership

Overview

Selecting the right vendor for your Microsoft Dynamics 365 Business Central implementation is a pivotal decision that can significantly impact the success of your project. In this chapter, the process of evaluating potential implementation partners and guide readers on making informed choices to ensure a successful partnership are explored.

A thorough evaluation framework is presented, encompassing considerations like experience in the field, expertise within the industry, feedback from clients, certifications, and the capabilities of customer support. Moreover, the significance of soliciting references and engaging in comprehensive interviews is underscored, aiming to glean insights into the implementation approach and track record of Solutions Partners for Business Applications.

After conducting thorough evaluations, readers will be equipped to make well-informed decisions. We offer guidance on selecting a vendor that aligns with the organization's culture, goals, and budget. Open communication and a collaborative approach are highlighted as crucial elements in building a strong and enduring partnership with the chosen vendor.

© Dr. Gomathi S 2024
Dr. Gomathi S, *Mastering Microsoft Dynamics 365 Business Central*,
https://doi.org/10.1007/979-8-8688-0230-0_3

Throughout the chapter, we present a clear roadmap outlining the step-by-step process of vendor selection to ensure a structured approach that minimizes the risk of mismatched partnerships. We also suggest the consideration of proof of concept or pilot projects with shortlisted vendors to assess their implementation capabilities in a real-world context.

By the end of this chapter, readers will have the knowledge and insights needed to embark on a partnership that can transform their organization through Microsoft Dynamics 365 Business Central implementation.

Introduction

Selecting the right vendor for your Microsoft Dynamics 365 Business Central implementation is a pivotal moment in your journey toward digital transformation. The choice you make can significantly influence the success of your project, affecting everything from the efficiency of your business operations to your bottom line. In this chapter, we embark on a crucial exploration: the process of evaluating potential implementation partners and, ultimately, choosing the right vendor.

When it comes to Business Central implementation, the marketplace is awash with vendors, each vying for your attention with promises of expertise and excellence. Yet, as an organization seeking a partner for this important venture, it's essential to navigate through this sea of options wisely. The key is to find a partner who not only possesses the technical know-how but also aligns with your unique business needs and vision. This chapter is your compass in that journey.

Your journey to Business Central implementation success begins with this chapter. By the end of it, you'll be equipped with the knowledge and insights needed to embark on a partnership that can transform your organization. So, let's embark on this crucial expedition together, navigating the path to selecting the perfect partner for your Microsoft Dynamics 365 Business Central implementation.

Choosing the Right Vendor

Having navigated the landscape of potential implementation partners and diligently evaluated their qualifications and capabilities, you've now reached a critical juncture in your Business Central implementation journey: the selection of the right vendor. In this section, we delve into the art and science of making this decision wisely, ensuring that your choice aligns seamlessly with your organizational culture, objectives, and budget.

Selecting the right vendor goes far beyond the transactional aspect of procurement. It is, in essence, the formation of a partnership that can either elevate your project to new heights of success or present unforeseen challenges. The vendor you choose should be more than just a supplier of services; they should become a strategic ally in your pursuit of digital transformation.

To guide you through this pivotal decision-making process, we offer valuable methods and techniques that will empower you to make a choice that is not only pragmatic but also visionary.

Alignment with Organizational Culture

Importance: Alignment with organizational culture is vital because it sets the tone for how well the vendor will integrate into your organization's working environment. It's about ensuring that the vendor's values, work ethics, and corporate culture resonate with your own. Here's why it is important:

a. **Collaboration and Productivity**: When a vendor aligns with your organizational culture, there is a higher likelihood of a seamless integration of their team with your own. Similar cultural values and work ethics can facilitate smoother collaboration, leading to increased productivity. For example, if your organization values transparency and open communication, a vendor who shares these values is more likely to foster an environment of trust and efficient information exchange.

b. **Reduced Conflict**: Misalignment in cultural values can lead to conflicts and misunderstandings. It's important to avoid situations where the vendor's approach and attitudes clash with those of your organization. This alignment helps minimize potential disputes and ensures a more harmonious working relationship.

c. **Employee Morale**: When a vendor's culture aligns with your organization's, it can positively impact your employees' morale. Employees are more likely to engage and cooperate with a vendor who fits into the existing culture, making the implementation process smoother and more enjoyable for all involved.

d. **Cultural Adaptation**: If a vendor understands and respects your organizational culture, they are more likely to adapt their strategies and methods to align with your unique needs. This adaptability can lead to a more tailored and effective implementation process.

Impact: The impact of alignment with organizational culture can be far-reaching and profound:

i. **Enhanced Communication**: When both parties share common values and communication styles, it becomes easier to convey ideas, expectations, and concerns. This leads to more effective communication, reducing the chances of misunderstandings and miscommunications during the implementation process.

ii. **Improved Problem-Solving**: A shared cultural foundation can foster a collaborative problem-solving environment. Vendors who understand your organization's culture are more likely to approach challenges with a mindset that aligns with your own, leading to more effective and creative solutions.

iii. **Long-Term Relationship**: A vendor who aligns with your organizational culture is more likely to view the relationship as a long-term partnership rather than a one-time transaction. This can result in continued support, ongoing innovation, and a vendor who is genuinely invested in your organization's success.

iv. **Employee Satisfaction**: When employees witness a vendor that seamlessly integrates into the organizational culture, it can boost their job satisfaction. This, in turn, can lead to a more engaged and motivated workforce, which is essential for the success of any implementation project.

Alignment with Objectives:

Assess whether the vendor's approach and solutions align with your project's objectives. The vendor should not merely provide a one-size-fits-all solution but should demonstrate a willingness to customize and tailor their services to your specific needs.

Importance: Alignment with objectives is of paramount importance in the vendor selection process because it ensures that the vendor's approach, solutions, and expertise align with the specific goals and objectives of your Business Central implementation. Here's why it is important:

1. **Goal Achievement**: Your organization embarks on a Business Central implementation to achieve specific goals, such as improving operational efficiency, increasing revenue, or enhancing customer satisfaction. The vendor you select should share a commitment to helping you achieve these goals. If there is alignment, the vendor will be more motivated to customize their services and solutions to meet your objectives effectively.

2. **Customization and Flexibility**: Every organization has unique needs and challenges. An aligned vendor is more likely to offer customized solutions tailored to your specific requirements, rather than providing generic, one-size-fits-all services. This customization can lead to a more successful implementation.

3. **Long-Term Success**: The alignment of objectives extends beyond the initial implementation phase. It is about ensuring that the vendor's partnership is geared toward long-term success and growth. A vendor who aligns with your objectives, leveraging innovative features such as the AI-driven Copilot in Dynamics 365 Business Central, is more likely to stay committed to your organization's ongoing

success. This not only enhances the efficiency of current processes but also positions your organization to adapt and thrive in the ever-evolving landscape of business technology.

Impact: The impact of alignment with objectives can be substantial and far-reaching:

1. **Efficient Implementation**: When the vendor's objectives are aligned with yours, their strategies and actions will be directed toward achieving your desired outcomes. This alignment streamlines the implementation process, reducing unnecessary delays and complications.

2. **Greater ROI**: An aligned vendor is more likely to deliver solutions and services that directly contribute to the achievement of your objectives. This can lead to a higher return on investment (ROI) as the implementation results in tangible benefits.

3. **Effective Problem-Solving**: Inevitably, challenges and obstacles will arise during the implementation process. When the vendor's objectives are in sync with yours, they are more likely to approach these challenges with a shared commitment to finding solutions that support your goals.

4. **Scalability**: As your organization evolves, your objectives may change. An aligned vendor is more likely to adapt and scale their services to meet your evolving needs, ensuring a continued positive impact on your business.

5. **Enhanced Collaboration**: When both parties share the same objectives, collaboration becomes more productive and meaningful. This can foster a sense of teamwork and shared responsibility, which is essential for a successful implementation.

6. **Value-Based Relationship**: An aligned vendor is not merely focused on completing a project but is genuinely invested in your organization's success. This can lead to a long-lasting, value-based partnership that extends beyond the initial implementation.

Budget Considerations: While cost is a significant factor, it should not be the sole determinant. Ensure that the vendor's pricing structure aligns with your budget, but also evaluate the value they bring to the table. A vendor that offers a slightly higher price but provides exceptional value and expertise may be a more prudent choice in the long run.

Importance: Budget considerations, in conjunction with alignment with objectives, are vital because they ensure that your vendor selection aligns with your financial constraints while still aiming to achieve your specific project objectives. Here's why this is important:

1. **Financial Viability**: Budget considerations help ensure that you choose a vendor whose pricing aligns with your allocated budget for the implementation. This is crucial to prevent overspending and financial strain during the project.

2. **Maximizing Value**: While cost is important, the focus should be on value rather than the lowest price. The vendor should offer a competitive price

that aligns with your budget while still providing the solutions and expertise necessary to achieve your project objectives effectively.

3. **Avoiding Overruns**: Aligning your budget with your objectives helps mitigate the risk of budget overruns. When your objectives are clear and budget constraints are understood, the vendor can provide a proposal that meets your requirements without unexpected costs arising during the implementation.

Impact: The impact of considering your budget in alignment with objectives is significant:

1. **Cost-Effective Solutions**: A vendor who understands your budget constraints and aligns their proposal with your objectives can provide cost-effective solutions that deliver maximum value for the allocated funds.

2. **Financial Stability**: Staying within budget is crucial to maintaining financial stability during and after the implementation. Effective budget management ensures that you have the resources needed for other critical aspects of your organization's operations.

3. **Clear Expectations**: Aligning your budget with objectives leads to clear expectations on both sides. The vendor knows what resources are available, and you know what outcomes to expect within the set budget, reducing the risk of misunderstandings or disputes.

4. **ROI Maximization**: When your budget aligns with your objectives, you can better assess the return on investment (ROI) of the implementation. This allows you to measure the success of the project in terms of achieving your specific goals while managing costs.

5. **Flexibility**: Understanding the budget constraints while pursuing your objectives allows for flexibility in decision-making. If necessary, adjustments can be made to the scope or timeline to stay within budget without compromising the achievement of critical objectives.

6. **Risk Mitigation**: By aligning your budget with objectives, you reduce the risk of financial strain or unexpected financial hurdles during the implementation. This mitigates the potential negative impacts on your organization's financial health.

Open Communication: Effective communication is the bedrock of a successful partnership. Evaluate the vendor's communication style and responsiveness. Are they receptive to your queries and concerns? Do they proactively keep you informed about project progress and potential challenges?

Importance: Open communication, combined with alignment with objectives, is of paramount importance because it ensures that there is clear and transparent dialogue between your organization and the selected vendor. Here's why this is important:

1. **Clarity of Objectives**: Open communication allows you to articulate your project objectives clearly to the vendor. It ensures that the vendor fully understands what you aim to achieve, reducing the risk of misinterpretation or misalignment.

2. **Realistic Expectations**: Through open communication, both parties can discuss the feasibility of objectives within the given constraints, such as budget and timeline. This dialogue helps set realistic expectations and avoids overambitious or unattainable goals.

3. **Issue Resolution**: Open communication channels create a platform for addressing challenges and issues as they arise during the implementation. This allows for swift problem-solving and minimizes the potential impact of obstacles on the project's progress.

4. **Adaptation to Changing Objectives**: Business Central implementations can be dynamic, and objectives may evolve over time. Open communication enables you to discuss and adapt to changes in objectives while keeping the vendor aligned with the new goals.

Impact: The impact of open communication with objectives is far-reaching:

1. **Goal Achievement**: When communication is open and transparent, it becomes easier to ensure that the vendor's efforts are directed toward achieving your objectives. Misunderstandings or deviations from the desired outcomes are less likely.

2. **Timely Issue Resolution**: Open communication facilitates the identification and resolution of issues in real-time. This prevents problems from escalating and causing delays or disruptions to the project.

3. **Improved Collaboration**: Effective communication fosters a sense of collaboration between your organization and the vendor. Both parties can work together as a cohesive team, sharing insights and expertise to achieve common goals.

4. **Risk Mitigation**: Transparent communication helps mitigate risks by addressing potential issues before they become major roadblocks. This reduces the likelihood of costly delays or project failures.

5. **Flexibility**: If your objectives change or if unexpected challenges arise, open communication enables you to adapt to these changes more effectively. It allows for a flexible project approach while ensuring alignment with your evolving goals.

6. **Trust Building**: Consistent open communication builds trust between your organization and the vendor. This trust is crucial for a successful and enduring partnership, as it promotes honesty, accountability, and a shared commitment to project success.

Collaborative Approach: Look for a vendor who embraces a collaborative approach. A willingness to work closely with your team and involve key stakeholders can lead to more effective problem-solving and knowledge transfer.

Importance: A collaborative approach, combined with alignment with objectives, is crucial because it fosters a sense of teamwork and shared responsibility between your organization and the selected vendor. Here's why this is important:

1. **Shared Responsibility**: Collaboration implies that both parties share responsibility for the success of the project. When the vendor is committed to your objectives and actively engages in the collaborative process, there's a greater sense of ownership and accountability.

2. **Knowledge Sharing**: Collaboration encourages the exchange of knowledge and expertise between your organization and the vendor. This sharing of insights can lead to innovative solutions and a deeper understanding of the project's objectives.

3. **Problem-Solving**: A collaborative approach means that both parties work together to identify and resolve challenges. This proactive problem-solving can prevent issues from escalating and disrupting the project's progress.

4. **Customization**: Collaborative vendors are more likely to tailor their services and solutions to meet your specific needs and objectives. This customization can lead to a more successful and impactful implementation.

Impact: The impact of a collaborative approach with objectives is substantial:

1. **Enhanced Creativity**: Collaboration encourages creative thinking and brainstorming. When both your organization and the vendor work together to achieve objectives, innovative ideas are more likely to emerge, leading to improved solutions and outcomes.

2. **Efficient Problem Resolution**: In a collaborative environment, issues and challenges can be addressed more efficiently. The combined expertise of both parties can lead to quicker problem resolution, minimizing the impact on the project's timeline and budget.

3. **Stronger Partnership**: A collaborative approach builds a stronger partnership between your organization and the vendor. This sense of partnership goes beyond the project's completion and can lead to continued support, future collaboration, and a shared commitment to long-term success.

4. **Adaptability**: Collaboration allows for greater adaptability when objectives change or new opportunities arise. The vendor is more likely to be flexible and responsive to evolving project goals.

5. **Knowledge Transfer**: When both parties actively collaborate, knowledge transfer occurs more naturally. This knowledge sharing can empower your organization to take ownership of the implemented solution and enhance internal capabilities.

6. **Reduced Risk**: A collaborative approach reduces the risk of misunderstandings and miscommunications. Clear and open communication within a collaborative partnership helps prevent misalignment with objectives.

Track Record: Examine the vendor's track record in delivering successful implementations. Request case studies or references from previous clients to gain insights into their ability to execute projects of a similar scope and complexity.

Importance: A vendor's track record, when considered alongside alignment with objectives, is important because it provides insight into their past performance and ability to meet specific project goals. Here's why this is important:

1. **Proof of Capability**: A vendor's track record demonstrates their capability to deliver successful projects. It serves as evidence of their experience and expertise in implementing solutions that align with client objectives.

2. **Risk Mitigation**: By examining a vendor's track record, you can assess their ability to manage risks effectively and avoid common pitfalls. A history of successful projects indicates a lower likelihood of issues that could jeopardize your implementation.

3. **Consistency**: A consistent track record of achieving project objectives suggests that the vendor has established reliable processes and practices for project management and goal attainment.

4. **Learning from Past Mistakes**: A vendor's track record can also reveal how they have learned from past mistakes. It shows whether they have a history of adapting and improving their approach to better align with client objectives over time.

Impact: The impact of considering a vendor's track record with objectives is substantial:

1. **Confidence in Success**: A strong track record instills confidence that the vendor can successfully execute your project in line with your objectives. This confidence can positively influence decision-makers and project stakeholders.

2. **Risk Reduction**: By selecting a vendor with a proven track record, you reduce the risk of project failure or deviations from objectives. The vendor's experience and expertise can help navigate potential challenges effectively.

3. **Efficient Goal Achievement**: A vendor with a history of aligning with client objectives is more likely to efficiently achieve your project goals. They understand the importance of delivering the desired outcomes.

4. **Better Resource Allocation**: With a vendor who consistently meets objectives, you can allocate resources more effectively, knowing that the project is on a path toward success. This can optimize budget and personnel allocation.

5. **Reputation and Credibility**: A vendor's track record contributes to their reputation and credibility in the industry. A positive track record can reflect well on your organization's choice of partner.

6. **Learning from Success**: Examining a vendor's successful projects from their track record can provide valuable insights into best practices and approaches that have yielded positive results for other organizations.

Choosing the Right Vendor

Having undertaken the diligent process of evaluating potential implementation partners, you now stand at a crucial crossroads: the selection of the vendor who will play a pivotal role in your Microsoft Dynamics 365 Business Central implementation. This section of the chapter is your guide to making this decision with wisdom and foresight.

Alignment with Organizational Culture, Goals, and Budget: One of the central themes in this phase is alignment. You will find that selecting the right vendor goes far beyond the transactional aspect of procurement. It's about choosing a partner whose values, work ethics, and corporate culture align seamlessly with your organization's ethos. Here, we explore three key facets of alignment:

1. **Culture Alignment:** The cultural fit between your organization and the chosen vendor is of paramount importance. A harmonious cultural alignment can foster a more productive and collaborative working relationship. When your vendor shares your values and work principles, it sets a strong foundation for mutual understanding and trust.

2. **Goal Alignment:** Your vendor should not merely provide a standardized solution; they should be committed to aligning their approach with your project's objectives. This entails understanding your specific goals and customizing their services to help you achieve those goals effectively.

3. **Budget Alignment:** While budget considerations are crucial, the focus should be on value rather than the lowest cost. The vendor's pricing structure should align with your budget, but you should also evaluate the value they bring to the table. Sometimes, a slightly higher upfront cost may lead to greater long-term value and efficiency.

Open Communication and Collaboration: Two additional pillars in selecting the right vendor are open communication and a collaborative approach. These aspects are essential for building a strong and enduring partnership. Effective communication and collaboration can have a profound impact on the success of your Business Central implementation. Here's why they matter:

- **Effective Communication:** The ability to communicate openly and transparently with your vendor is vital. It ensures that expectations are clear, questions are answered promptly, and issues are addressed in a timely manner. Effective communication minimizes misunderstandings and contributes to project efficiency.

- **Collaborative Approach:** Collaboration means that your vendor is not just a service provider but a partner who actively engages with your team. A collaborative vendor is open to working closely with your staff and involving key stakeholders in decision-making processes. This teamwork can lead to more effective problem-solving and knowledge transfer.

Tip for Vendor Selection

"Look for a vendor who demonstrates a strong commitment to understanding your business processes and customizing the solution to meet your specific needs."

As you navigate the vendor selection process, keep this tip in mind: "Look for a vendor who demonstrates a strong commitment to understanding your business processes and customizing the solution to meet your specific needs." This commitment to tailoring their services to your unique requirements is a sign of a vendor who is genuinely invested in your organization's success.

This tip is a crucial guiding principle when choosing the right vendor for your Microsoft Dynamics 365 Business Central implementation. Here's a more in-depth explanation of why this commitment is essential and how it can impact your project:

1. **Understanding Your Business Processes:**

   - **Importance:** Business Central implementation is not a one-size-fits-all endeavor. Your organization has unique business processes, workflows, and requirements. A vendor who invests time and effort in understanding these intricacies gains valuable insights into your operations.

   - **Impact:** When a vendor thoroughly understands your business processes, they are better equipped to tailor the solution to your specific needs. This leads to a more efficient and effective implementation, as the solution aligns seamlessly with your existing workflows.

- **Benefits:** In-depth knowledge of your business processes enables the vendor to identify opportunities for automation, optimization, and efficiency improvements. The result is a solution that not only meets your objectives but also enhances your daily operations.

2. **Configuring the Solution:**

- **Importance:** Configurations within Dynamics 365 Business Central fall under the domain of the functional consultant. This is critical as it allows for the alignment of the system with the unique business needs of the organization. The functional consultant, armed with an understanding of both the software and the business processes, plays a key role in tailoring configurations to enhance the system's relevance to specific requirements.

- **Impact:** The impact of functional consultants overseeing configurations is significant. By directly connecting business needs with system settings, these experts ensure that Dynamics 365 Business Central becomes a finely tuned instrument that resonates with the organization's operational nuances. This alignment minimizes disruptions, fostering a harmonious integration of the system into everyday workflows.

- **Benefits:** Handled by the functional consultant, configurations pave the way for numerous benefits. The system, finely configured to match specific business requirements, becomes a strategic asset. This approach supports sustained cost-effectiveness, heightened productivity, and a competitive advantage. As the organization evolves, configurations orchestrated by the functional consultant allow the system to adapt and grow organically, offering continuous support for ongoing success and providing a solid foundation for continuous improvement.

3. **Customizing the Solution:**

    - **Importance:** Generic, off-the-shelf solutions may not fully address your organization's unique requirements. A commitment to customization means that the vendor is willing to adapt and configure the Business Central system to match your specific needs.

    - **Impact:** Customization ensures that the implemented solution doesn't disrupt your existing processes but rather enhances them. It minimizes the need for workarounds or manual adjustments and allows your team to work more efficiently within the system.

    - **Benefits:** With a customized solution, you can achieve a higher degree of user adoption and satisfaction. Your staff will find it easier to embrace the new system when it aligns closely with their familiar processes and workflows.

4. **Tailored Solution for Success:**

- **Importance:** A vendor who customizes the solution is not just focused on completing a project; they are invested in your organization's success. Their commitment goes beyond the implementation phase and extends to the long-term benefits of the solution.

- **Impact:** A tailored solution is more likely to achieve your project objectives effectively. It provides the flexibility to adapt to changing business requirements and grow with your organization.

- **Benefits:** Over time, a customized solution can lead to cost savings, improved productivity, and a competitive advantage. It becomes a valuable asset that supports your organization's growth and evolution.

Role-Play Interview Scenario: Putting Theory into Practice

As we've explored the essential elements of vendor selection and partnership, it's crucial to not only understand these concepts in theory but also apply them in practical scenarios. To facilitate this learning process, we've designed a role-play interview scenario that allows you to step into the shoes of a decision-maker responsible for vendor selection. In this scenario, you will have the opportunity to engage in a simulated interview with a hypothetical vendor representative.

The Value of Role-Play: Role-playing provides a valuable opportunity to put your knowledge to the test and refine your skills in real-world situations. By participating in this interview scenario, you can practice asking relevant questions, evaluating a vendor's alignment with your objectives, and assessing their commitment to understanding your business processes and customizing the solution to meet your specific needs. It's a chance to experience firsthand the dynamics of a vendor-client interaction and gain insights into effective communication and collaboration. Afterward, we encourage you to reflect on the experience and share your observations, as this practical exercise will deepen your understanding of the vendor selection process and enhance your ability to make well-informed decisions that align with your organization's goals.

Scenario Description

In this role-play scenario, you will take on the role of a decision-maker responsible for vendor selection, while a colleague or peer will act as the vendor representative. The objective is to simulate an interview setting where you evaluate the vendor's suitability for your Microsoft Dynamics 365 Business Central implementation project.

Sample Interview Questions:

1. **Vendor Background and Experience:**

    - Can you provide an overview of your company's experience in implementing Microsoft Dynamics 365 Business Central?

    - Have you worked with organizations similar to ours in terms of industry and size?

2. **Alignment with Objectives:**

   - How do you typically approach understanding a client's specific objectives for an implementation project?

   - Can you share examples of how you've aligned your services with a client's unique project goals in the past?

3. **Communication and Collaboration:**

   - Describe your approach to communication during an implementation project. How do you keep clients informed about progress and challenges?

   - How do you encourage collaboration between your team and the client's team to ensure project success?

4. **Customization and Tailoring:**

   - How do you approach customizing the Microsoft Dynamics 365 Business Central solution to meet a client's specific needs and business processes?

   - Can you provide examples of how you've tailored solutions for clients with unique requirements?

5. **Problem-Solving and Issue Resolution:**

   - How do you handle unexpected challenges or roadblocks that may arise during an implementation project?

   - Can you share a specific instance where you successfully resolved a significant issue during a project?

6. **References and Track Record:**

   - Could you provide references from past clients who have undergone Microsoft Dynamics 365 Business Central implementations with your assistance?

   - What notable achievements or successful outcomes have you had in recent implementations?

7. **Budget and Cost Management:**

   - How do you typically structure pricing and budget considerations for your projects?

   - Can you discuss your approach to managing costs and ensuring that projects stay within budget?

8. **Post-implementation Support:**

   - What types of post-implementation support and maintenance services do you offer?

   - How do you ensure that clients receive ongoing support and assistance after the implementation is complete?

9. **Cultural Fit and Partnership Building:**

   - How do you assess whether there is a cultural fit between your organization and the client's organization?

   - Can you describe your approach to building strong and enduring partnerships with clients?

10. **Adaptability and Future-Readiness:**

- How do you ensure that the solutions you implement remain adaptable to changing business needs and evolving technologies?

- Can you provide examples of how you've helped clients future-proof their systems?

Note   A detailed list of Sample Interview Questions is provided in Appendix B.

Contractual Considerations

Licensing Sales Contract

When entering into the realm of Microsoft Dynamics 365 Business Central implementation, having a robust Licensing Sales Contract is paramount. This agreement outlines the terms and conditions surrounding the licensing of the software, ensuring a clear understanding of the permissions, limitations, and obligations associated with its usage. It acts as a foundational document, setting the stage for a transparent and mutually beneficial relationship between your organization and the vendor.

Deployment Contract

The Deployment Contract is a comprehensive document that outlines the roadmap for the implementation journey. It includes crucial deliverables such as fictional requirement documents, technical requirement documentation, solution blueprints, training manuals, integration architectures, and more. Equally important are the billing milestones, providing a structured approach to financial engagements throughout the deployment phase. This contract serves as a guide, ensuring that expectations are aligned, and both parties are committed to the successful implementation of Dynamics 365 Business Central.

Ongoing Support Contract

Beyond implementation, the Ongoing Support Contract is a vital component of the vendor-client relationship. It defines the service times, Service Level Agreements (SLAs), and payment options for continuous support and maintenance. This contract ensures that your organization receives the necessary assistance and troubleshooting promptly, contributing to the long-term success and sustainability of your Dynamics 365 Business Central solution.

Intellectual Property of Customizations

Addressing the Intellectual Property (IP) of customizations is a critical aspect of vendor contracts. This section clarifies the ownership and rights associated with any customizations made to the Dynamics 365 Business Central solution. Clear delineation of IP ensures that your organization retains control over tailored solutions, fostering flexibility and independence.

Exit Options and Ownership of Code

The Exit Options and Ownership of Code section is a safeguard mechanism. It delineates the terms under which your organization can part ways with the vendor if necessary. Understanding the exit options and having clarity on code ownership ensures a smooth transition in case of any unforeseen circumstances or changes in partnership dynamics.

Best to Address During Vendor Selection

These contractual aspects are best addressed during the vendor selection process. Proactively discussing and aligning on these terms can prevent potential pitfalls and ensure that your organization doesn't get locked into an unfavorable arrangement. It lays the groundwork for a transparent and collaborative vendor-client relationship, setting the stage for success in Dynamics 365 Business Central implementation.

Microsoft BizApps Ecosystem

Experience with other products in the Microsoft BizApps Ecosystem is a pivotal factor in vendor selection. Dynamics 365 Business Central is part of the Biz Apps Suite, and anticipating future projects, such as Sales Force Automation, Customer Service Automation, or Marketing Automation, is prudent. A vendor capable of not only Dynamics Business Central but also CRM modules becomes a strategic partner for the long-term journey of your organization. Their familiarity with the broader Microsoft BizApps Ecosystem ensures a seamless integration of various solutions, providing a holistic approach to your organizational needs.

Microsoft Ecosystem

In addition to Dynamics 365 Business Central, a vendor's experience with products like Power Platform (Power BI, Power Apps, Power Automate) is a critical differentiator. As analytics emerges as a likely next project, having a partner well-versed in the Microsoft Ecosystem ensures a cohesive and integrated approach. Being with the same partner across different projects in the Microsoft Ecosystem offers a great starting point, fostering continuity, consistency, and efficiency in your organization's technological journey.

Why It Matters

Imagine a scenario where your organization is not just looking for a Dynamics 365 Business Central implementation but also considering future projects such as enhancing data analytics, automating workflows, or developing custom applications. This is where the broader Microsoft Ecosystem, encompassing Power BI, Power Apps, and Power Automate, becomes crucial.

Example

Let's say your next project involves harnessing advanced analytics to derive actionable insights from your business data. Having a vendor with expertise in Power BI, a powerful business analytics tool, ensures a seamless integration between your Dynamics 365 Business Central data and a sophisticated analytics platform. The vendor's familiarity with the Microsoft Ecosystem allows them to leverage Power BI's capabilities effectively, providing your organization with robust reporting and analytics capabilities.

Scenario

Consider a scenario where your organization aims to streamline and automate certain business processes. A vendor well-versed in Power Automate can design automated workflows that connect seamlessly with your Dynamics 365 Business Central solution. This expertise facilitates the creation of efficient and customized workflows, reducing manual interventions and enhancing overall operational efficiency.

Benefits

Having a vendor experienced in the Microsoft Ecosystem brings several benefits. Firstly, there's a natural synergy between different Microsoft tools, enabling a smooth flow of data and processes. Secondly, your organization benefits from a consistent user experience across various Microsoft applications, promoting user adoption and minimizing training requirements. Lastly, a vendor with a holistic understanding of the Microsoft Ecosystem can offer integrated solutions that address multiple facets of your business needs.

Digital Transformation: A Journey Toward Organizational Evolution

Digital transformation is not merely an expected outcome; it's a dynamic and ongoing process that orchestrates the evolution of an organization in the digital age. Picture it as a journey, a continuous exploration of technological advancements and strategies aimed at enhancing efficiency, agility, and overall performance. In simple terms, it's the organization's quest to leverage cutting-edge technologies to revolutionize its operations and achieve strategic objectives.

Example Scenario: Enhancing Supply Chain Visibility in Manufacturing

Consider a manufacturing company embarking on its digital transformation journey. By integrating advanced technologies, such as IoT sensors and real-time data analytics, into its supply chain, the organization achieves a substantial improvement in supply chain visibility. This means the company can now track and manage inventory, monitor production processes, and anticipate potential disruptions in real-time. The outcome? Enhanced efficiency, reduced costs, and a competitive edge in the market.

Embracing Digital Transformation: A Holistic Approach

Digital transformation is not a one-time achievement; it's an ongoing commitment to staying at the forefront of technological advancements. Beyond the buzzword, it's about creating a culture of innovation and adaptability within the organization. Whether it's automating manual processes, embracing data-driven decision-making, or enhancing customer experiences, digital transformation is about aligning technology with strategic goals.

Importance

Emphasizing the importance of digital transformation during the vendor selection process is paramount. It ensures that your chosen partner understands the broader context and is equipped to guide your organization on this transformative journey.

Impact

A vendor well-versed in digital transformation can help you navigate complexities, identify opportunities for innovation, and implement solutions that align with your organization's long-term vision.

Benefits

Ultimately, embracing digital transformation yields benefits beyond immediate outcomes. It positions your organization for sustained growth, adaptability to market changes, and a competitive advantage in the ever-evolving digital landscape. By understanding digital transformation as a holistic journey, you set the stage for a successful partnership that goes beyond implementation, fostering continuous evolution and excellence.

Conclusion

In the quest for a successful Microsoft Dynamics 365 Business Central implementation, the selection of the right vendor and the establishment of a strong partnership are paramount. This chapter has taken you on a journey through the intricacies of vendor selection, emphasizing the need for a holistic approach that considers multiple factors while keeping your project objectives at the forefront.

We've explored the critical importance of alignment—alignment with your organizational culture to foster collaboration and shared values, alignment with your project objectives to ensure your vendor's efforts are directed toward your desired outcomes, and alignment with your budget constraints to optimize cost-effectiveness. Additionally, we've highlighted the significance of open communication and a collaborative approach, which promote transparency, creativity, and efficient problem-solving.

By considering a vendor's track record and evaluating their past performance in relation to achieving objectives, you can make an informed decision that reduces risk, instills confidence, and sets the stage for a successful partnership.

Selecting the right vendor is not merely a transaction but the foundation of a strategic alliance. The vendor you choose should be more than a service provider; they should be a committed partner on your journey toward digital transformation. Remember that the success of your Business Central implementation is not solely about the technology but about the collaboration, communication, and alignment between your organization and your chosen vendor.

As you proceed with your implementation project, carry forward the knowledge and insights gained in this chapter. Apply the methods and techniques discussed here to ensure that your partnership with the selected vendor is one that not only meets your immediate objectives but also lays the groundwork for long-term success.

Exercise

1. Choose a vendor who has implemented Business Central solutions in your industry or a related industry. What were the key objectives of their projects, and were they successful?

2. Analyze client testimonials or case studies to assess the vendor's performance. What strengths and weaknesses can you identify from their track record?

3. How might the insights gained from analyzing a vendor's track record influence your own vendor selection process for a Business Central implementation project?

CHAPTER 4

Project Management Methodologies

Embarking on a journey with Microsoft Dynamics 365 Business Central is a strategic voyage through the complex realms of business processes. This chapter steers you through the sea of project management methodologies, highlighting the importance of the right approach for successful implementation. Here, we delve into Microsoft's methodologies: the traditional yet comprehensive Sure Step and the innovative Success by Design, launched in 2023. While Sure Step offers a well-established route, Success by Design provides a flexible and adaptive approach, essential for navigating the evolving needs of modern businesses. These methodologies act as your navigational stars, guiding you toward a successful deployment of Business Central and ensuring a journey that is both effective and efficient.

In recent years, the landscape of project management methodologies in ERP implementations has witnessed a significant evolution. Agile methodologies, once considered unsuitable for the structured world of ERP, are now gaining increasing relevance. This shift reflects a growing recognition of Agile's flexibility and adaptability, making it an invaluable tool in responding to the dynamic demands of modern business environments. As we explore the traditional Waterfall and the emerging Agile approaches, we see a paradigm shift toward methodologies that can accommodate rapid changes and iterative development, even in the complex arena of ERP systems.

© Dr. Gomathi S 2024
Dr. Gomathi S, *Mastering Microsoft Dynamics 365 Business Central*,
https://doi.org/10.1007/979-8-8688-0230-0_4

The process of determining the most appropriate methodology, whether Agile or Waterfall, can be likened to the act of selecting the optimal sail for a journey. Would you choose the conventional, robust, and linear approach of Waterfall methodology, which is tailored for a well-defined and static objective? Alternatively, would you go for the Agile methodology, characterized by its flexible and adaptable approach that enables fast adjustments in response to evolving business demands?

Gaining a comprehensive understanding of the extent of your journey, including the objectives and results of the project, is crucial for determining the trajectory. Similar to the practice of charting celestial bodies for navigational purposes, the act of defining the project scope serves as a guiding framework for the undertaking, enabling all those involved in the endeavor to comprehend the intended trajectory.

In addition, the allocation of an appropriate crew with well-defined responsibilities is of equal importance to staffing a ship with experienced seafarers. The successful coordination and synchronization of a crew's efforts in propelling a ship forward with precision and harmony can be achieved through the allocation of resources and the establishment of clear team responsibilities.

This chapter serves as a comprehensive resource for making informed decisions regarding these crucial matters. By utilizing the information presented in this document, you will possess the necessary knowledge to strategically plan and execute a successful deployment of Business Central, resulting in a very successful outcome.

Agile Methodology

The Agile approach encompasses a project management and product development philosophy that places significant emphasis on flexibility, customer satisfaction, iterative progress, and the capacity to adapt to evolving requirements during the course of a project. The system is constructed upon the basis of joint endeavor and is distinguished by the partitioning of tasks into brief periods of work, accompanied by regular evaluation and adjustment of strategies.

The fundamental principles of Agile are rooted in the Agile Manifesto, which places importance on the following:

- The prioritization of individuals and interactions over processes and tools

- The prioritization of functional software development over extensive documentation

- The prioritization of customer participation over contract negotiation

- Adapting to change as opposed to adhering to a predetermined plan

The ideals, which have their roots in the field of software development, can be effectively applied to various projects, including the implementation of Business Central.

The use of Agile methodology for Business Central: The incorporation of Agile methodologies in the context of a Business Central project necessitates the assimilation of Agile concepts and their subsequent use throughout the different phases of the implementation procedure. The following approach can be employed:

1. **Commence with Agile Training:** Ensure that your team is well-versed in Agile methodologies and principles, including Scrum and Kanban, prior to commencing. Acquaint individuals with Agile artifacts and ceremonies, including sprints, stand-ups, and retrospectives, as well as the product backlog, sprint backlog, and increments.

2. **Formulate the Project's Objectives and Vision**:
   Assist stakeholders in elucidating the Business
   Central implementation's overarching vision.
   Establish a clear definition of success and effectively
   convey this vision to the team.

3. **Establish the Product Backlog**: Create a list of
   all features, functions, and prerequisites for the
   Business Central system, in order of importance to
   the organization. This document is in a constant
   state of evolution as the initiative advances.

4. **Provide a Definition of Sprints**: Typically, the
   project should be divided into sprints, which are
   time-boxed periods lasting two to four weeks. It is
   recommended that every iteration be assigned a
   specific set of deliverables that can be completed
   within its designated time period.

5. **Iterative Development**: A subset of the items
   from the product backlog should be chosen for
   development during each iteration. Deliver a
   product increment that is potentially shippable at
   the conclusion of each iteration.

6. **Foster Collaboration**: Consistent engagement with
   stakeholders guarantees that the product proceeds
   in accordance with user feedback, whereas daily
   stand-up meetings facilitate team cohesion.

7. **Demonstrate Adaptability**: Acquire feedback
   during every sprint review and be ready to
   modify the product backlog and subsequent
   sprints accordingly. This flexibility is an essential
   component of Agile.

8. **Emphasize Continuous Improvement**: Conduct a retrospective meeting at the conclusion of each iteration to evaluate the progress made and identify areas for improvement. Implement these insights in subsequent cycles.

9. **Deploy Phased Features**: Opt for a phased implementation strategy in which the complete Business Central solution is launched simultaneously. This would enable users to acclimatize to the system gradually and provide avenues for feedback and enhancement.

10. **Embracing Change**: In the event that business requirements evolve throughout the project, the adaptable characteristics of Agile enable a revaluation of priorities and a course correction to be executed with minimal disruption.

Adapting Agile to Business Central and ERP Implementations

Recent insights, such as those from McKinsey, have shed light on how Agile can be successfully adapted to the unique challenges of ERP implementations. Agile in this context brings several benefits:

Faster Pace and Greater Transparency: Agile methodologies enable a more rapid progression of project phases in ERP implementations, offering greater transparency at each step. This approach allows for quicker decision-making and more timely critical interventions.

Early Realization of Business Value: By breaking down the ERP implementation into smaller, manageable increments, Agile allows organizations to realize business value earlier in the process, as opposed to waiting until the end of a lengthy project.

High-Level Scope with Flexibility for Refinement: While Agile in ERP requires a high-level scope definition upfront, it retains the flexibility for detailed scope refinement and prioritization as the project progresses. This approach ensures that while the overarching goals are clear, there is room to adapt to changing needs and insights.

Implementing an ERP system, such as Microsoft Dynamics 365 Business Central, requires a thoughtful approach that considers the interdependencies between various modules and functionalities. For instance, the General Ledger, a fundamental part of accounting, relies on a well-defined chart of accounts, which itself is influenced by requirements from Sales, Purchases, Manufacturing, Retail, and other areas.

Addressing ERP-Specific Challenges with a Hybrid Approach

Implementing core ERP components like the General Ledger often requires a more structured approach due to interdependencies with other modules. In such cases, blending Agile practices within a broader Waterfall framework can offer the best of both worlds: the flexibility of Agile within each module and the structured approach of Waterfall to manage dependencies. This hybrid strategy allows businesses to leverage Agile's benefits while ensuring a cohesive and comprehensive ERP implementation.

Waterfall Method: Contrasting with Agile in ERP

The Waterfall model, a mainstay in the realm of software development and project management, is characterized by its linear and sequential design approach. Each phase in this model—Requirements, Design, Implementation, Verification, and Maintenance—must be completed before the next one begins. This method is often seen as rigid and structured, where scope, budget, and timelines are firmly set from the outset, and deviations are less accommodated compared to Agile methodologies.

Core Principles of Waterfall

1. **Sequential Phases**: The Waterfall model is divided into distinct phases such as Requirements, Design, Implementation, Verification, and Maintenance. Each phase commences solely upon the completion of the preceding phase.

2. **Thorough Documentation**: In accordance with the linear nature of the process, it is imperative to have extensive documentation at each phase to ensure that all stakeholders have a clear understanding of every facet of the project.

3. **Project Scope Clarity**: The Waterfall model is most effective when applied to projects that possess a precisely defined scope that is improbable to evolve throughout its course.

4. **Predictability**: The Waterfall model provides a notable degree of predictability, particularly for projects characterized by unambiguous technical specifications, owing to its well-organized structure.

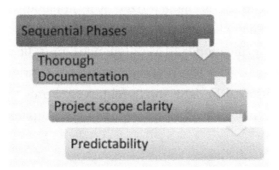

Figure 4-1. *Phases of Waterfall*

Implementing Waterfall for Business Central

In the context of Business Central implementation, the Waterfall model that is depicted in Figure 4-1 generally entails the subsequent stages:

1. **Gathering and Documenting Requirements**: Perform an exhaustive examination of business processes and system prerequisites. This will require stakeholders to participate in in-depth discussions to determine the scope of the Business Central implementation and to ascertain their requirements.

2. **System Design**: Convert the intricate specifications into an all-encompassing system design. This would entail delineating the architecture of Business Central, encompassing its integration with pre-existing systems and databases.

3. **Execution**: Construct the system in adherence to the design specifications. During this stage, tasks such as configuring Business Central, customizing features, and developing any necessary add-ons or integrations would be undertaken.

4. **Verification**: Conduct exhaustive performance, security, and functionality tests on the Business Central implementation. Conducting testing guarantees that every requirement that was recorded during the initial phase has been fulfilled.

5. **Deployment**: Once verified, the complete system is deployed to the live environment. This is typically a single, planned event where the switch from the old system to Business Central occurs.

6. **Maintenance**: After deployment, the system enters the maintenance phase where it is routinely updated, bugs are fixed, and new features can be added as required.

However, as highlighted in the McKinsey article, the Agile methodology has been increasingly adapted for ERP implementations, challenging the traditional dominance of Waterfall in this field. Agile, with its iterative and flexible nature, offers several advantages in the dynamic landscape of ERP:

Adaptability to Change: Unlike Waterfall, Agile is designed to accommodate and respond to changes in requirements, even late in the project lifecycle.

Incremental Delivery: Agile breaks down the ERP implementation into smaller, manageable increments, allowing for earlier testing, feedback, and adjustments.

Stakeholder Engagement: Agile methodologies emphasize continuous stakeholder involvement throughout the project, ensuring that the final product aligns more closely with user needs and expectations.

In contrast to the sequential and rigid structure of Waterfall, Agile methodologies offer a more dynamic and responsive approach to ERP implementation. This adaptability is particularly beneficial in complex ERP projects where requirements may evolve, and new needs emerge as the project progresses.

Choosing the Right Approach for ERP Implementation

While Waterfall provides a structured and predictable framework, ideal for projects with fixed requirements and clear deliverables, Agile offers flexibility and responsiveness, crucial for adapting to changing business needs in ERP implementations. The choice between Waterfall and Agile – or a hybrid approach that combines elements of both – depends on the specific requirements, complexity, and context of the ERP project at hand.

Agile vs. Waterfall: Choosing the Right Approach

Table 4-1 serves as a comparative guide between two prominent project management methodologies, Agile and Waterfall, particularly in the context of implementing Microsoft Dynamics 365 Business Central (BC). It is designed to highlight key differences in project structure, flexibility, client involvement, and various other aspects critical to managing and executing a Business Central implementation project.

Each column contrasts how Agile and Waterfall address these aspects, providing concrete examples to illustrate the practical implications of choosing one methodology over the other. The aim is to assist decision-makers in determining which approach aligns best with their project goals, organizational culture, and specific needs of the Business Central system they are planning to deploy.

Table 4-1. *Agile vs Waterfall Method*

Aspect	Agile	Waterfall	Example
Project Structure	Iterative and incremental	Linear and sequential	**Agile:** Developing a custom report for BC is done in short sprints with feedback loops **Waterfall:** The entire BC system's reporting module is built before moving to testing
Flexibility	High flexibility to adapt to changes	Limited flexibility, changes can be costly	**Agile:** Requirements for BC modules can evolve during the project **Waterfall:** BC requirements must be set in detail from the start
Client Involvement	Requires client involvement throughout the project	Client involvement mainly at milestones	**Agile:** The client regularly reviews iterations of the BC implementation **Waterfall:** The client reviews the BC system after deployment

(*continued*)

Table 4-1. (*continued*)

Aspect	Agile	Waterfall	Example
Risk Management	Continuous risk management	Risk is typically assessed at the beginning and at major milestones	**Agile:** If a feature in BC isn't working well, it can be revised in the next sprint **Waterfall:** If BC's inventory module doesn't meet needs, revisions will require significant rework after its completion
Time to Delivery	Potentially faster initial delivery of usable systems	Longer time until delivery of a fully functional system	**Agile:** A basic version of BC goes live quickly for immediate use **Waterfall:** BC is only fully deployed after all modules are tested and completed
Budgeting	Budgeting is iterative and can change with scope	Budget is fixed based on detailed initial estimates	**Agile:** Costs for BC are revisited each sprint, adjusting for added features **Waterfall:** The total cost for BC implementation is agreed upon in advance

(*continued*)

Table 4-1. (*continued*)

Aspect	Agile	Waterfall	Example
Documentation	Documentation is lean and updated throughout	Comprehensive documentation is created early on	**Agile:** Documentation for BC user stories evolves with each sprint **Waterfall:** A complete specification for the BC system is produced before development starts
Quality Assurance	Ongoing through the project lifecycle	Usually performed after the build phase before deployment	**Agile:** BC features are continuously tested and improved **Waterfall:** BC undergoes a full testing phase after all development is completed
Scope	Scope can change during the project	Scope is defined upfront, and changes are discouraged	**Agile:** Additional BC features can be added mid-project as needed **Waterfall:** All BC features are defined before the project starts; changes require formal change requests

(*continued*)

Table 4-1. (*continued*)

Aspect	Agile	Waterfall	Example
Outcome Predictability	Less predictable, adapts to emerging outcomes	More predictable, if the initial plan is accurate	**Agile:** The end state of BC adapts to business needs throughout the project **Waterfall:** The BC system is expected to match the initial project scope and design
Team Dynamics	Requires cross-functional, self-organizing teams	Relies on specialized teams working in silos	**Agile:** A BC project team may handle multiple aspects like development, testing, and deployment **Waterfall:** Separate BC teams handle each project phase sequentially
Suitability	Suited for projects where requirements are expected to change	Suited for projects with well-understood requirements	**Agile:** Ideal for a BC roll-out in a new market with evolving needs **Waterfall:** Ideal for a BC upgrade where requirements are clear and stable

Implementing an ERP System: A Hybrid Agile-Waterfall Approach

When embarking on the implementation of an enterprise resource planning (ERP) system, such as Microsoft Dynamics 365 Business Central, organizations often face the challenge of balancing the need for structured planning with the flexibility to adapt to evolving requirements. This is where a hybrid Agile-Waterfall approach becomes particularly valuable.

The Hybrid Approach: Combining Structure with Flexibility

In traditional ERP implementations, the Waterfall model has been the go-to approach due to its linear and structured nature. It allows for comprehensive planning and clear milestones, which are crucial in complex ERP projects. However, the rigidity of this model can be a limitation, especially in today's dynamic business environments where requirements can change rapidly.

To address this, many organizations are now adopting a hybrid approach that combines the structured planning of Waterfall with the flexibility and adaptability of Agile methodologies. This approach allows for the comprehensive planning and clear milestones of Waterfall, while also incorporating the iterative development and responsiveness of Agile.

In this hybrid model, the project is initiated with a Waterfall approach, where the overall scope, major milestones, and architecture of the ERP system are defined. This initial phase sets a clear direction and lays the groundwork for the project. Once this foundation is established, the project shifts to an Agile mode for the development and deployment phases. This shift allows for iterative development, where modules or features of the ERP system are developed, tested, and refined in short cycles or sprints.

Phased Implementation: Rolling Out ERP in Stages

A key aspect of this hybrid approach, as highlighted in the McKinsey article, is the concept of phased implementation. Instead of deploying the entire ERP system in one go, it is rolled out in stages, module by module. This staged rollout allows organizations to manage the complexity of ERP implementation more effectively and reduces the risks associated with a full-scale deployment.

For example, in a manufacturing organization, the implementation might start with the financial modules, such as General Ledger, Accounts Payable, and Inventory Management. Once these core financial components are successfully implemented and stabilized, the project can then move on to more complex modules like Manufacturing and Supply Chain Management. This phased approach not only ensures a smoother implementation process but also allows users to gradually adapt to the new system, thereby enhancing the overall acceptance and effectiveness of the ERP solution.

A Balanced Approach for ERP Success

By combining the structured planning of Waterfall with the iterative and flexible nature of Agile, the hybrid approach offers a balanced and effective strategy for ERP implementation. It accommodates the need for comprehensive planning and control, while also providing the agility to respond to changing requirements and business needs. The phased implementation further supports this by allowing organizations to manage the complexity of ERP projects, ensuring a smoother transition and greater success in the long run.

Which One to Choose?

Choosing the right project management methodology for a Microsoft Dynamics 365 Business Central (BC) implementation depends on various factors, including the organization's culture, the complexity and size of the project, regulatory considerations, and the need for flexibility in responding to change.

Agile Methodology for Business Central: If the Business Central implementation requires frequent changes based on user feedback, or if the project needs to adapt to evolving business processes, Agile could be the more appropriate choice. Agile allows for iterative releases, which can be particularly beneficial for a BC implementation that's expected to evolve over time. This approach would enable the organization to start using the core functionalities of BC quickly and refine the system through continuous improvement.

Waterfall Methodology for Business Central: For organizations with well-defined processes and requirements that are unlikely to change, or in industries with heavy regulations that require extensive documentation and clear audit trails, the Waterfall methodology might be more appropriate. If the scope of the BC implementation is clear and stable, and the stakeholders prefer a planned and phased approach with fixed budgets and timelines, then Waterfall could offer the structure and predictability needed.

Hybrid Approach: There are scenarios where a hybrid approach, combining elements of both Agile and Waterfall, could be beneficial for a BC implementation. For example:

- Use the Waterfall model for the initial stages of the project where requirements gathering, scoping, and high-level design are completed.

- Shift to an Agile approach during the development and deployment phases to accommodate changes and improve through iterations.

Other Methodologies: Apart from Agile and Waterfall, there are other project management methodologies like PRINCE2 (Projects IN Controlled Environments) or the PMI's PMBOK (Project Management Body of Knowledge) that provide frameworks which can be adapted to the needs of a Business Central implementation.

PRINCE2 is a process-driven project management method, which emphasizes dividing projects into manageable and controllable stages. It's widely recognized in the UK and internationally, especially in government and IT sectors.

PMBOK is a set of standard terminology and guidelines for project management, which is more a knowledge base than a methodology, but it can be applied to the Business Central implementation through the creation of custom processes.

Considerations for Choosing a Methodology

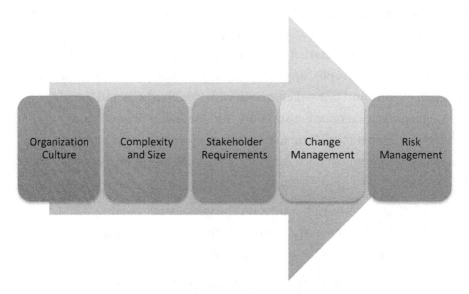

Figure 4-2. Key considerations before choosing a methodology

- **Organizational Culture:** The company's culture and how teams are used to working can greatly influence the effectiveness of the chosen methodology.

- **Complexity and Size:** The complexity and size of the project may dictate a need for more (or less) structure.

- **Stakeholder Requirements:** How stakeholders engage with the project team and how frequently their input is needed.

- **Change Management:** How well the organization can handle change and how often requirements are expected to evolve.

- **Risk Management:** The organization's appetite for risk and the need for risk mitigation strategies.

Figure 4-2 shows the key consideration before choosing the methodology. Choosing between Agile and Waterfall for a Business Central implementation is a strategic decision that should align with the project's objectives, organizational workflow, and stakeholder expectations. Each approach has its strengths and ideal use cases, and sometimes a hybrid model is best suited to balance the benefits of both.

Finally, there isn't a one-size-fits-all approach to a Business Central implementation. The decision should be based on a thorough assessment of project-specific factors and organizational dynamics. It's also common for organizations to seek the advice of a BC consultant or implementation specialist to identify the best methodology to use, drawing on their experience with past implementations.

Project Scope and Deliverables

Defining the project scope and deliverables is a critical early step in any project, including the implementation of Microsoft Dynamics 365 Business Central. This process involves establishing clear and precise boundaries for what the project will encompass and the specific outcomes it will produce.

Project Scope

The project scope articulates the boundaries of the project. It spells out the features, functionalities, and processes that will be included in the implementation of Business Central.

The project scope serves as a critical document that delineates the project's limits and objectives. It comprehensively outlines the features, functionalities, and processes that will be encompassed within the Business Central implementation. Equally vital, it defines what falls outside the scope to mitigate scope creep—the risk of the project expanding beyond its initial boundaries.

While Agile methodologies often encourage the consideration of new requirements, it's important to strike a balance when operating within a traditional Waterfall framework. In this context, the project scope provides a valuable tool for managing expectations and ensuring that project objectives remain clear and achievable. By embracing Agile principles selectively, organizations can accommodate evolving requirements while maintaining control over the project's overall scope and goals.

Components of Defining Project Scope

1. **Goals and Objectives:** Clearly define what the implementation of Business Central aims to achieve. This might include improved efficiency, better data analytics, or enhanced customer service.

2. **Functional Requirements:** Detail the specific requirements that Business Central must meet, which may involve accounting features, inventory management, or CRM functionalities.

3. **Project Deliverables:** List the tangible outputs, such as configured modules, custom reports, user training programs, and support materials.

4. **Milestones:** Establish key points in the project timeline when certain parts of the project will be completed.

5. **Constraints:** Recognize the limitations related to budget, time, or resources that may impact the project.

6. **Assumptions:** Note any assumed factors upon which the project plan is based, like the availability of data or integration capabilities with existing systems.

7. **Exclusions:** Define what is explicitly outside the project's scope, such as legacy system retirement or non-BC related processes.

Deliverables

Deliverables are the tangible and intangible outcomes that the project will produce. In the context of a Business Central implementation, deliverables might include

- A fully configured and operational Business Central environment

- Customized modules and extensions to meet the unique needs of the business

- Data migration from legacy systems into Business Central

- Training materials and sessions for end users

- Post-deployment support agreements

Creating a Scope Statement

To formalize the project scope, a scope statement is drafted. This document should be clear, concise, and understood by all stakeholders. It acts as a reference point throughout the project to ensure that work aligns with the agreed objectives and to manage changes effectively.

Managing Scope and Deliverables:

Throughout the project, it is vital to manage the scope and deliverables diligently. This involves

- Monitoring work to ensure alignment with the scope

- Controlling changes through a formal change management process

- Validating and accepting deliverables through quality assurance processes

Note   For your convenience and to ensure that this guide remains streamlined and focused on key methodologies, the comprehensive checklist for "Defining Project Scope and Deliverables" has been included as Appendix C. This checklist serves as a practical tool to assist in meticulous planning and execution of your Microsoft Dynamics 365 Business Central implementation. Please refer to Appendix C at the end of this book for the detailed checklist, which can be used as a step-by-step reference throughout your project journey.

Resource Allocation and Team Roles in Business Central Implementation

The success of any Microsoft Dynamics 365 Business Central (BC) implementation heavily depends on the strategic alignment and optimization of two critical aspects: resource allocation and team roles. These components are the backbone of project management, ensuring that the right people with the right skills are working on the right tasks at the right time.

Resource Allocation: Resource allocation in a BC implementation involves distributing the available resources in an efficient manner to support project activities. It's essential for maintaining a balance between the workload and the available workforce, while also managing the budget and timelines. Effective resource allocation maximizes productivity, reduces downtime, and increases the chances of project success by ensuring that all tasks have the necessary personnel and tools for completion.

Team Roles: Team roles are equally pivotal. They define the structure of the project team and clarify the responsibilities and expectations for each member. Understanding and clearly defining team roles is fundamental for effective collaboration and communication. It aids in the identification of expertise areas, delineation of accountability, and supports a coordinated approach to tackling project challenges.

Potential Teams in a Business Central Implementation

Implementing Business Central typically involves the coordination of multiple teams, each with specific roles and responsibilities:

1. **Steering Committee:**

    - Senior Management

    - Project Sponsors

2. **Project Management Team:**

    - Project Manager

    - Scrum Master (for Agile methodology)

    - Business Analyst

3. **Technical Team:**

    - Solution Architect

    - Developers

    - Database Administrators

    - IT Security Specialists

4. **Functional Team:**

    - Functional Consultants

    - Subject Matter Experts (SMEs)

    - System Users

5. **Quality Assurance Team:**

   - Test Managers

   - Testers

6. **Training and Support Team:**

   - Trainers

   - Documentation Specialists

   - Support Technicians

7. **Change Management Team:**

   - Change Managers

   - Communication Officers

8. **External Stakeholders:**

   - Vendors

   - Consultants

Key Roles and Their Importance

Each team contributes uniquely to the BC implementation:

- **Steering Committee:** Provides strategic direction, secures funding, and ensures the project aligns with business objectives

- **Project Management Team:** Oversees the project's overall execution, ensuring that it is completed on time, within budget, and to the desired quality standards

- **Technical Team:** Handles all technical aspects, from system architecture to software development and database management, ensuring the system is robust, secure, and scalable

- **Functional Team:** Translates business requirements into system configurations, ensuring the solution meets the business processes it is intended to support

- **Quality Assurance Team:** Ensures the solution is tested and that any defects are identified and corrected, guaranteeing the system is reliable and user-ready

- **Training and Support Team:** Prepares training materials and conducts sessions to ensure end users are proficient in using the new system and provides ongoing support post-implementation

- **Change Management Team:** Manages the human side of change, ensuring that the organization and its employees are ready for the new system, thus facilitating a smoother transition

- **External Stakeholders:** Provide additional expertise, support, and services that might not be available in-house

Resource allocation and team roles must be defined early and reviewed regularly throughout the project to respond to any changes. A BC implementation is a dynamic project; as such, the allocation of resources and roles might need to adapt to project phase changes, milestones reached, or unexpected challenges. It's this flexibility, combined with a strong foundational understanding of each team's contribution, that propels a Business Central implementation toward success.

Table 4-2. *Team Roles and Responsibilities*

Team/Role	Responsibilities	Example
Steering Committee	• Set strategic direction, approve budgets • Monitor project progress • Resolve high-level issues	Approving the increased budget for additional customizations requested by the user team
Project Management Team	• Plan and oversee project execution • Manage timelines and budgets • Communicate with stakeholders • Mitigate risks	Using Gantt charts to track project milestones and adjust schedules as needed
Project Manager	• Coordinate all project activities • Lead planning and implementation 1. Serve as the point of contact for stakeholders	Leading weekly status meetings to keep the project on track
Scrum Master (Agile)	• Facilitate Agile ceremonies • Assist the team in following Agile practices 1. Remove impediments	Conducting daily stand-ups to check progress and address any blockers
Business Analyst	• Elicit and analyze requirements • Document processes 1. Act as a liaison between stakeholders and technical team	Creating a detailed business process flow that guides system configuration

(continued)

Table 4-2. (*continued*)

Team/Role	Responsibilities	Example
Technical Team	• Design system architecture • Develop custom solutions • Manage databases and integrations 1. Ensure system security	Designing a scalable architecture that supports expected transaction volumes
Solution Architect	• Define overall system design • Ensure technical solutions align with business goals a. Oversee development and infrastructure teams	Specifying the use of Azure services for hosting the Business Central environment
Developers	• Customize and configure BC environment • Write code for additional functionalities • Fix bugs	Developing a custom module for advanced inventory management
Database Administrators	• Manage database systems • Ensure data integrity and security 1. Optimize database performance	Regularly backing up the Business Central database and optimizing indexes
IT Security Specialists	• Secure the system against threats • Manage user access and authentication 1. Monitor system for security breaches	Implementing multi-factor authentication for system access

(*continued*)

Table 4-2. (*continued*)

Team/Role	Responsibilities	Example
Functional Team	• Map business processes to BC capabilities • Configure BC according to needs 1. Validate system functionality against requirements	Configuring Business Central to match the client's procurement workflow
Functional Consultants	• Customize BC functionalities • Provide expertise on modules 1. Assist with data migration	Setting up and testing the Accounts Payable module
Subject Matter Experts (SMEs)	• Provide detailed knowledge on business processes • Assist in requirement gathering and testing 1. Help with training material	Guiding the setup of financial reporting based on industry best practices
System Users	• Test system functionalities • Provide feedback on usability • Identify any process gaps	End users testing the order-to-cash cycle to ensure it meets their day-to-day needs
Quality Assurance Team	• Plan and execute tests • Document test cases and results • Ensure that the solution meets quality standards	Performing stress testing to ensure system performance under load

(*continued*)

Table 4-2. (*continued*)

Team/Role	Responsibilities	Example
Test Managers	• Oversee testing efforts • Ensure test coverage 1. Report on testing progress and outcomes	Compiling test reports to highlight areas of concern for the development team
Testers	• Execute test plans, record defects • Verify fixes	Systematically testing purchase order processing and recording any issues
Training and Support Team	• Develop training programs • Conduct training sessions • Provide post-implementation support	Creating user manuals and conducting workshops for the sales team on the new system
Trainers	• Teach system functionality • Customize training materials to user roles • Assess user competence	Leading hands-on training sessions in Business Central's customer relationship module
Documentation Specialists	• Create and maintain system documentation • Develop help guides and FAQs • Ensure documentation is accessible and up-to-date	Writing a comprehensive user guide that accompanies each training module
Support Technicians	• Resolve user issues • Maintain system post-implementation • Provide technical assistance	Troubleshooting login problems for users after system go-live

(*continued*)

Table 4-2. (*continued*)

Team/Role	Responsibilities	Example
Change Management Team	• Develop change management plans • Communicate changes to stakeholders • Support employees through the transition	Running communication campaigns to build positive anticipation for the new system
Change Managers	• Manage change initiatives • Track employee engagement • Mitigate resistance to change	Organizing focus groups to gather employee feedback on the upcoming changes
Communication Officers	• Oversee internal communications • Keep all stakeholders informed • Produce informational materials	Creating newsletters and intranet posts about the implementation progress
External Stakeholders	• Provide specialized services and products • Offer expertise and external perspectives • Support implementation with additional resources	A third-party add-on vendor providing a specialized tax calculation service for BC

Each role and team's responsibilities in Table 4-2 are illustrative and might vary depending on the organization's size, structure, and specific needs during the Business Central implementation.

Conclusion

The exploration of project management methodologies in the context of Business Central implementation reveals a landscape where both structure and flexibility are paramount. The structured waters of the Waterfall approach offer clear milestones and a predictable path, while the Agile methodology brings adaptability and responsiveness to change, qualities increasingly essential in dynamic business environments.

Insights from recent analyses, such as those presented in the McKinsey article, highlight the successful application of Agile in ERP contexts. This evolving landscape emphasizes the importance of selecting a project management approach that aligns with the specific needs and complexities of ERP projects. The choice between the structured predictability of Waterfall and the adaptive agility of Agile should be informed by the unique demands and context of each ERP implementation.

Defining project scope and deliverables requires meticulous planning and clear communication. These practices are crucial in setting the stage for success, ensuring a shared understanding among all stakeholders of the project's goals and expected outcomes.

Resource allocation and defining team roles are critical aspects of project execution. The right combination of people, skills, and resources can significantly influence the project's trajectory, turning potential challenges into opportunities for success. In Business Central implementations, assembling a team that is technologically proficient and attuned to the business processes the system will support is vital.

Deciding on a project management approach is not about adopting a universal solution; it involves understanding and responding to the specific needs and context of the organization. For Business Central implementations, this might mean adopting a hybrid model that combines the structured approach of Waterfall with the iterative advantages of Agile. Such a model ensures strategic alignment while maintaining the flexibility to adapt to user feedback and evolving requirements.

In conclusion, the success of a Business Central implementation hinges on careful planning, effective resource management, and the ability to adapt to new insights and changing business landscapes. With these components in place, organizations are better equipped to navigate the complexities of ERP implementation, emerging with robust solutions that meet and exceed their business needs.

KEY HIGHLIGHTS

- Agile vs. Waterfall methodologies: Agile is flexible and iterative; Waterfall is structured and sequential.

- Project scope definition is crucial for setting boundaries and expectations.

- Detailed deliverables outline what the project will specifically achieve.

- Effective resource allocation ensures optimal use of personnel and tools.

- Clear team roles facilitate collaboration and define responsibilities.

- Teams in Business Central implementations include Project Management, Technical, Functional, QA, Training, and Change Management.

- Hierarchical structure of teams ranges from Steering Committee to External Stakeholders.

- The right methodology and proper planning are key to successful Business Central implementation.

EXERCISE

Project Scenario 1: Rapidly Evolving Tech Startup

A tech startup is planning to implement Business Central to keep up with its rapid growth. The company anticipates frequent changes to its processes and needs a system that can adapt quickly.

Task: Decide whether Agile or Waterfall is more suitable and justify your choice.

Project Scenario 2: Large Financial Institution with Strict Compliance

A large bank with stringent regulatory requirements is implementing Business Central to integrate its financial processes. The project must adhere to a variety of compliance standards and the scope is well-defined.

Task: Decide whether Agile or Waterfall is more suitable and justify your choice.

Project Scenario 3: Retail Chain for Inventory Management

A retail chain requires a Business Central implementation for better inventory management across its multiple locations. The core requirements are known, but the client wants the flexibility to adjust features based on seasonal sales data.

Task: Decide whether Agile or Waterfall is more suitable and justify your choice.

Project Scenario 4: Manufacturing Company Modernizing Legacy Systems

A manufacturing company with legacy systems is looking to modernize its ERP with Business Central. The scope is extensive and includes migrating decades of data.

Task: Decide whether Agile or Waterfall is more suitable and justify your choice.

Project Scenario 5: Non-Profit Organization with Limited Budget

A non-profit organization with a limited budget needs a clear upfront cost for a Business Central implementation. They require a straightforward solution with no significant changes anticipated.

Task: Decide whether Agile or Waterfall is more suitable and justify your choice.

Project Scenario 6: Government Department with Fixed Deadlines

A government department has to implement Business Central within a fiscal year to comply with new regulations. The deadline is immovable, and the project scope is subject to public procurement rules.

Task: Decide whether Agile or Waterfall is more suitable and justify your choice.

Project Scenario 7: International Corporation with Diverse Stakeholder Groups

An international corporation is rolling out Business Central to unify processes across global offices. There are many stakeholder groups with different needs, and the company expects to iterate on the implementation based on feedback from various regions.

Task: Decide whether Agile or Waterfall is more suitable and justify your choice.

CHAPTER 5

Data Migration and Cleaning

The importance of efficient data transfer and cleaning becomes increasingly significant as firms undergo modernization, particularly in the implementation of intricate systems such as Business Central. Data migration encompasses more than the mere transfer of data from one system to another. The undertaking in question is a strategic venture that necessitates meticulous planning, implementation, and supervision. The process encompasses the extraction, cleaning, confirmation, and transfer of data, aiming not only to achieve effective migration but also to enhance compliance with the new system. The primary objective is to enhance the quality and use of data, hence enabling more precise and well-informed company insights and decision-making processes.

An important part of the transfer process is data cleaning, which means carefully going through the data to find and fix any mistakes, inconsistencies, or duplicates. This is done to keep the quality and reliability of the material. This plan also makes sure that data protection and security rules are followed, which is very important in today's data-driven world. The steps of transferring data and cleaning it up are both very important for making a Business Central rollout work. With these methods, companies can get the most out of their data assets.

Dr. Gomathi S, *Mastering Microsoft Dynamics 365 Business Central*, https://doi.org/10.1007/979-8-8688-0230-0_5

In this chapter of the Business Central implementation guide, three critical components for integrating data into a new system are described in detail. Data Migration Planning which is depicted in Figure 5-1, Data Cleaning and Validation, and Data Security and Privacy are among these elements.

During this discourse, we shall examine the fundamental techniques and facets that necessitate due consideration in order to plan the data migration process in an appropriate manner. This entails establishing specific objectives, comprehending the extent of the data that needs to be transmitted, and formulating an all-encompassing migration plan that incorporates timetables, allocation of resources, and risk mitigation.

In this chapter, we will know the methodologies employed to evaluate the integrity of pre-existing data and the approaches utilized to cleanse it in preparation for its integration into Business Central. During this presentation, we shall examine the significance of data validation, the methodologies employed to guarantee the precision and uniformity of data, and the approaches utilized to sustain data quality by implementing continuous improvement practices.

In addition to these processes, a critical factor in the success of data migration for ERP systems, like Dynamics 365 Business Central, is the alignment of the migration timeline with the company's financial calendar. This is where the timing of ERP go-live becomes paramount, as most ERP migrations, including Business Central, are strategically planned to go live at the beginning of a financial year. For instance, if a financial year runs from April 2023 to March 2024, the data as of 31st March 2023 becomes a pivotal point.

This timing is essential to ensure a seamless transition, enabling companies to start their new financial year with a fresh, updated system. It also plays a significant role in the financial audit processes that typically follow the closure of the fiscal year, necessitating the need for audit entries in both the old system and Dynamics 365 Business Central.

Given the specific data sets for migration, such as Master Data (Customers, Vendors, Items, etc.), Opening Balances (Debtors, Creditors, Inventory), and Open Transactions (Open POs, Sales Orders, etc.), careful planning and synchronization are required. The Opening Balances in the Trial Balance, for example, must match the Open Transactions and Item Stock values. In cases involving manufacturing, additional data elements like Open Production Orders and Work in Progress accounts also need careful alignment with the Trial Balance. The preparation of these data sets often takes several days, highlighting the client preparation time needed before migration can commence.

Understanding the complexities of these processes and the time investment required both from the client's side and the vendor's side is crucial. Often, this is where most of the project time is invested, and it becomes the single most common reason for project delays. Acknowledging the vendor's role and timeframe is essential, as the vendor needs a few days to effectively bring the data into Dynamics Business Central.

To mitigate these challenges, innovative approaches such as using Power BI on current ERP systems are recommended. This allows for a detailed analysis of historical data, reducing the need for transferring extensive historical records and focusing instead on migrating only the most crucial and recent open transactions. Such strategies not only streamline the migration process but also significantly reduce the associated costs and complexities, making the transition to Dynamics 365 Business Central more efficient and manageable.

We will conclude by discussing the critical significance of data privacy and security throughout the migration process. An overview of methodologies pertaining to the interpretation of data protection legislation, the implementation of secure migration procedures, the management of access restrictions, and the maintenance of security and compliance within the Business Central environment will be presented in this chapter.

Planning for Data Migration

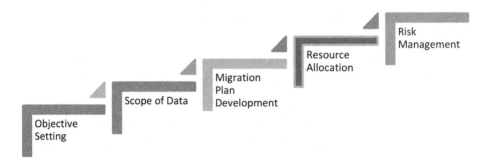

Figure 5-1. *Key steps for planning data migration*

Crucial Aspects to Consider

1. **Objective Setting:**

    - Define the goals of the migration clearly.

    - Align migration objectives with broader business goals.

2. **Scope of Data:**

    - Identify which data sets need to be migrated.

    - Determine the relevance and necessity of each data set to the new system.

3. **Migration Plan Development:**

    - Create a detailed migration plan outlining every phase of the process.

    - Include timelines, milestones, and deliverables.

4. **Resource Allocation:**

- Assess and procure the necessary resources, encompassing software, hardware, and personnel, in order to fulfill the project requirements.

- Develop a comprehensive strategy to ensure enough training and support is provided to all members of the team.

5. **Risk Management:**

- The objective is to perform a risk assessment in order to identify potential challenges that may develop throughout the process of relocation.

- Develop mitigation strategies for identified risks.

Roles in Data Migration

1. **Technical Consultant:**

- Responsible for the technical aspects of the migration, such as data extraction, transformation, and loading (ETL).

- Ensures that the technical infrastructure is in place and that the data migration tools are correctly configured.

- Addresses technical challenges and customizes solutions to fit the unique needs of the project.

2. **Functional Consultant:**

- Focuses on the business side, ensuring that the data migration aligns with business processes and requirements.

- Validates that the migrated data works well within Business Central, facilitating user acceptance testing.

- Acts as a liaison between the business stakeholders and the technical team.

Other Stakeholders Involved

1. **Project Manager:**

- Oversees the entire migration project, ensuring it stays on track and within budget.

- Communicates with all stakeholders and resolves conflicts.

2. **Data Owners/Custodians:**

- Provide insights into the data's business context and usage.

- Help in defining data quality standards and validation checks.

3. **Quality Assurance Team:**

- Responsible for the validation and verification of the migrated data.

- Ensures that the data is accurate and that the migration adheres to predefined quality standards.

4. **IT Security Specialist:**

- Ensures that the migration process is secure and that data privacy regulations are followed.

- Implements data protection strategies and monitors for potential security breaches.

5. **End Users:**

- Provide feedback on the data's functionality within the new system.

- Involved in user acceptance testing to ensure the data meets their daily operational needs.

The Migration Process Explained

1. **Pre-migration Planning:**

- Assess current data quality, define data standards, and prepare the data for migration.

- Develop a backup strategy to protect existing data.

2. **Migration Execution:**

- Execute the migration according to the plan, using ETL tools to move the data.

- Apply data validation and cleaning processes during the transfer.

3. **Post-migration Activities:**

- Conduct thorough testing with the help of end users to ensure data integrity and functionality.

- Train users and provide documentation on the new system's data environment.

4. **Continuous Monitoring and Support:**

- Monitor the system post-migration to quickly address any data issues or user concerns.

- Offer ongoing support and maintenance to ensure the stability and reliability of the migrated data.

Microsoft's Migration Tools

Direct Migration from Well-Known ERPs

Microsoft offers migration tools for direct data transfer from popular ERP systems like QuickBooks to Dynamics 365 Business Central. This facilitates an efficient migration process, especially for standard data sets. For more details on this, Microsoft provides guidance, as seen in the documentation for migrating from QuickBooks to Dynamics 365 Business Central.

Microsoft Rapid Start Services

The Rapid Start Services provided by Microsoft are a crucial resource in the migration process. They assist in simplifying the setup of new companies in Business Central, including the configuration of tables and data migration. The tool is especially helpful in streamlining the process of importing data into Business Central.

Configuration Packages

Configuration packages in Business Central allow for an efficient way to import and export data. These packages can be used to import data from legacy systems into Business Central, helping in organizing data into a format compatible with Business Central's tables.

Templates for Data Capture

Microsoft also offers templates for data capture, which can be used to gather the necessary data before migration. These templates are particularly useful for ensuring that all relevant data fields, including any custom fields added by vendors, are accounted for in the migration.

Utilizing these Microsoft-provided tools can significantly streamline the migration process, ensuring that data is transferred efficiently, accurately, and securely to Business Central. It's advisable for both functional and technical consultants to familiarize themselves with these tools to enhance the effectiveness of the migration strategy.

Note   A detailed checklist for the planning and execution of data migration, tailored for both functional and technical consultants, is provided in Appendix D for your convenience and comprehensive guidance.

The success of a data migration initiative is contingent upon the meticulous planning and coordinated efforts of the project team. Within this team, functional and technical consultants have distinct yet complementary responsibilities that ensure a smooth transition to Business Central. The following table provides a structured checklist that delineates these roles across various stages of the migration process. Functional consultants focus on aligning the migration with business objectives and processes, while technical consultants manage the technical execution and integrity of the data migration. Table 5-1 serves as a detailed guide to assist both consultants in fulfilling their respective duties effectively.

This guide shows you which styles you should use for the content of your chapters. You can paste your chapter text here, or write straight into the template.

Table 5-1. *Migration Responsibilities for Functional and Technical Consultants*

Aspect	Functional Consultant Responsibilities	Technical Consultant Responsibilities
	Pre-migration	
Objective Setting	Align data migration objectives with business goals and engage stakeholders to define migration scope and priorities	Evaluate existing technical infrastructure and requirements for Business Central implementation
Data Analysis	Identify and categorize data sets for migration; review data quality and structure in current systems	Assist in data quality assessment and prepare data extraction procedures from legacy systems
Process Mapping	Map business processes and define how each data type will be used in Business Central	
Compliance and Regulation	Ensure understanding of data protection laws and define data privacy requirements for migration	Plan for data security during migration, implementing encryption and secure transfer protocols

(continued)

Table 5-1. (*continued*)

Aspect	Functional Consultant Responsibilities	Technical Consultant Responsibilities
Migration Planning		
Data Migration Plan	Develop a detailed data migration plan with timelines and milestones; coordinate with the technical consultant for technical feasibility	Set up and configure data migration tools; develop custom scripts or programs if necessary
Data Cleaning	Define data cleaning requirements; supervise the data cleaning process to maintain data integrity	
User Training and Documentation	Plan for end-user training and prepare user documentation and data dictionaries	Document the technical details of the migration process and ensure technical documentation is updated
During Migration		
Testing	Coordinate user acceptance testing (UAT) to ensure the new system meets business needs; verify data integrity and quality post-migration	Perform data extraction, transformation, and loading (ETL); monitor the migration process and troubleshoot issues
Change Management	Manage communication with business users about changes and address their concerns and feedback	Implement automated checks to verify data during migration; collaborate with the functional consultant on data validation

(*continued*)

Table 5-1. (*continued*)

Aspect	Functional Consultant Responsibilities	Technical Consultant Responsibilities
Post-migration		
Validation and Sign-Off	Validate that the migrated data meets all business requirements and obtain sign-off from stakeholders	Conduct system testing to ensure technical performance and rectify any technical issues identified
Support and Optimization	Provide post-migration support to users and optimize business processes based on new data insights	Provide technical support during the stabilization period and assist in resolving post-migration technical issues
Backup and Recovery		Establish a comprehensive backup strategy for the migration and plan for recovery actions in case of migration failure

Data Cleaning and Validation

Data Cleaning and Validation are pivotal in ensuring the integrity and utility of data in any system, especially when migrating to a platform like Business Central. The process not only improves the quality of the data but also fortifies its reliability for future business operations and analysis.

Data Cleaning: A Multi-Step Approach

1. **Data Audit:**

   - **Technique:** Utilize statistical analysis and data profiling tools to scrutinize the current data. Look for patterns, anomalies, outliers, and any inconsistencies that could indicate data quality issues.

   - **Responsibility:** It's the duty of the functional consultant to define what constitutes data quality within the business context, while the technical consultant executes the statistical analysis and profiling, interpreting the data findings.

2. **Workflow Specification:**

   - **Technique:** Establish clear rules for data transformation and correction. This could involve setting up data standardization parameters, such as uniform date formats or consistent capitalization.

   - **Responsibility:** The functional consultant will create the rules based on business requirements, and the technical consultant will translate these rules into executable actions or scripts.

3. **Workflow Execution:**

   - **Technique:** Deploy both automated processes (like scripts for bulk updates) and manual interventions for more nuanced or complex data issues that automated tools cannot accurately resolve.

- **Responsibility:** Technical consultants handle the execution, using tools and scripts to cleanse the data. They work closely with functional consultants, who may need to review exceptions and guide the decision-making process for complex data issues.

4. **Post-Cleaning Analysis:**

   - **Technique:** After cleaning, employ a mix of reconciliation techniques and data quality metrics to ensure the data aligns with the intended quality standards.

   - **Responsibility:** Functional consultants verify that the cleansed data meets business needs, while technical consultants provide reports and evidence of the improvements and validate the technical accuracy.

Data Validation: Ensuring Data Meets Business and Technical Standards

1. **Data Screening:**

   - **Technique:** Implement automated validation tools that screen the data against predefined rules. This step often involves checking data types, ranges, uniqueness, and format consistency.

   - **Responsibility:** Technical consultants configure and manage the validation tools, whereas functional consultants define the validation criteria based on business rules.

2. **Data Verification:**

- **Technique:** Perform manual sampling where random data sets are checked for accuracy. Use cross-system verification to ensure consistency across different databases or systems.

- **Responsibility:** Functional consultants lead this manual verification process, often involving users who understand the data's business context, while technical consultants facilitate the comparison through system queries and reports.

3. **Rule Conformance:**

- **Technique:** Apply constraint-based validation, such as database constraints, and pattern matching using regular expressions to ensure data entries conform to business logic.

- **Responsibility:** The functional consultant sets up the business logic rules, and the technical consultant implements these rules at the database or application level.

4. **Referential Integrity Checks:**

- **Technique:** Use database management systems' built-in referential integrity constraints to ensure foreign keys correctly reference primary keys in related tables.

- **Responsibility:** The technical consultant ensures that the referential integrity is maintained technically. In contrast, the functional consultant understands and dictates the business relationships that these data integrity checks must support.

A Collaborative Endeavor

Data Cleaning and Validation are not solitary activities; they require a symbiotic relationship between the technical know-how of the technical consultants and the business acumen of the functional consultants. The functional consultant defines what clean and valid data looks like from a business perspective, sets the standards, and communicates the business logic. The technical consultant then translates these needs into actions, using a variety of tools and techniques to ensure the data is fit for use in Business Central.

Ultimately, the goal of this collaboration is to transform raw data into a strategic asset that drives informed decision-making and efficient business processes in the new Business Central environment.

Data Security and Privacy in Data Migration

When undertaking the migration of data to Business Central, ensuring the security and privacy of data is not just a best practice; it's an imperative governed by an array of compliance regulations and ethical considerations.[1] This segment of the migration process demands a vigilant approach to protect sensitive information from unauthorized access or breaches during and after the transition.

---

[1] www.nimble.com/blog/the-crm-evolution-top-trends-to-watch-in-2024/

Understanding the Landscape of Data Security and Privacy

Before we dive into the practicalities, it's crucial to understand the landscape. Data security involves protecting digital data from unauthorized access, while privacy ensures that personal information is used in accordance with the preferences of the individual and the law.[2]

Key Considerations for Data Security and Privacy

1. **Regulatory Compliance:**

   - Familiarize yourself with laws like the General Data Protection Regulation (GDPR) in the EU, the California Consumer Privacy Act (CCPA),[3] and other local data protection regulations.

   - **Example:** Under GDPR, if you're migrating data that includes information on EU citizens, you need to ensure that data is handled according to the principles of the regulation, such as data minimization and purpose limitation.

2. **Data Classification and Handling:**

   - Classify data according to sensitivity and apply appropriate handling procedures for each class.

   - **Example:** Customer credit card information is classified as highly sensitive and must be encrypted both at rest and in transit during migration.

---

[2] https://pib.gov.in/PressReleasePage.aspx?PRID=1642422
[3] https://staging.dxc.com/nz/en/insights/customer-stories/westpac-new-zealand-limited-leverages-microsoft-power-platform

3. **Risk Assessment:**

    -   Conduct a thorough risk assessment to identify and mitigate potential security threats.

    -   **Example:** Identify risks such as potential data leaks during the migration and establish encryption protocols to mitigate them.

Techniques and Measures for Ensuring Data Security and Privacy

1. **Data Masking:**

    -   Use data masking techniques to hide sensitive information, ensuring that during testing and development, the privacy of the data subjects is maintained.

    -   **Example:** Masking out portions of social security numbers in a testing environment.

2. **Encryption:**

    -   Encrypt data before it's migrated to protect it from interception during transit.

    -   **Example:** Utilizing end-to-end encryption methods when transferring data to Business Central.

3. **Access Controls:**

    -   Implement strict access controls and permissions to ensure only authorized personnel can access sensitive data.

- **Example:** Setting role-based access controls in Business Central to restrict access to employee salary details.

4. **Audit Trails:**

   - Maintain audit trails to record access and changes to data, providing accountability and traceability.

   - **Example:** Using Business Central's logging capabilities to track who accessed customer data and when.

Responsibilities in Data Security and Privacy

- **Functional Consultant:**

  - Ensure that data handling complies with legal and business policy requirements.

  - Work with stakeholders to understand the data privacy needs and translate these into technical requirements.

- **Technical Consultant:**

  - Implement the technical solutions like encryption, data masking, and access controls.

  - Ensure that the migration tools and processes adhere to the security and privacy specifications.

Post-migration Data Security and Privacy

Once the data is in Business Central, the journey isn't over. Maintaining data security and privacy is an ongoing process.

1. **Continuous Monitoring:**

   - Regularly monitor the system for any unusual activity or breaches.

   - **Example:** Setting up security incident and event management (SIEM) systems to monitor and alert on suspicious activities.

2. **Regular Audits:**

   - Conduct periodic audits to ensure compliance with data security policies and regulations.

   - **Example:** Performing quarterly audits to review access logs and verify compliance with data handling policies.

3. **Data Retention and Deletion:**

   - Establish policies for data retention and ensure that data is not kept longer than necessary. Implement secure deletion practices.

   - **Example:** Implementing data lifecycle management policies in Business Central that automatically delete customer records after a certain period.

In essence, security and privacy are not merely about compliance; they're about building and maintaining trust—trust with customers, employees, and business partners. This trust is foundational to the success of any business operation in the modern data-driven landscape. Through careful planning, execution, and ongoing vigilance, businesses can ensure that their data migration to Business Central not only enhances their operational capabilities but also upholds the high standards of data security and privacy that stakeholders expect.

Conclusion

Concluding the chapter on Data Migration and Cleaning for Business Central implementation, it is recognized that data migration represents a significant undertaking. It's not merely a technical task but a considerable business initiative that demands extensive resources, affecting cost, project duration, and client satisfaction.

The chapter initially emphasized the importance of comprehensive planning in data migration. This phase is crucial for setting the stage for a smooth transition. The process requires a collaborative effort where functional and technical consultants come together, merging their distinct expertise to fulfill both business and technological requirements, ensuring a migration plan that is robust, efficient, and minimizes risks.

In the segment on data purification and validation, various methodologies were discussed to ensure data integrity and quality, which are vital for making informed decisions. The combination of a functional consultant's grasp of business rules and a technical consultant's expertise in data transformation is key to achieving high-quality data integration into Business Central.

Furthermore, the chapter addressed the essential principles of data security and privacy, especially critical in an environment where data breaches can severely affect trust and compliance. A comprehensive checklist was presented to protect sensitive information throughout the migration process, highlighting the need to maintain data security and privacy.

Incorporating tools, techniques, and features of Dynamics 365 Business Central into the migration strategy is crucial. Executing the migration aligned with the financial year's start can be strategically beneficial. This approach not only makes the chapter more relevant to Business Central but also provides insightful guidance for vendor selection, determining the scope of data migrations, validating migrated data, and planning project milestones.

A recommended strategy is to utilize Power BI on existing ERP systems to extract insights from historical data, which can significantly streamline the data migration process by focusing primarily on migrating open transactions. This method can greatly reduce the complexities and resource demands of data migration, making it a more manageable and cost-effective endeavor.

In summary, the process of data migration underscores the significance of data as a key business asset. The methodologies, roles, and checklists detailed in this chapter, combined with the strategic application of Business Central's tools and Power BI for data analysis, aim to safeguard this asset. They ensure that the outcome of the migration process is a secure, dependable, and valuable Business Central implementation, establishing a solid foundation for business operations in the digital era.

KEY HIGHLIGHTS

- Strategic planning is crucial for successful data migration to Business Central, requiring clear objectives and risk mitigation strategies.

- Functional consultants must ensure the migration aligns with business processes, while technical consultants handle the technical aspects.

- Data cleaning and validation are essential for maintaining data integrity, involving techniques like profiling, manual reviews, and automated checks.

- Data security and privacy must be prioritized, with adherence to laws like GDPR and methods such as encryption and access controls.

EXERCISE

Objective: Apply the principles of data migration planning, data cleaning and validation, and data security and privacy to a real-world scenario.

Scenario:

You are the lead consultant for a mid-sized retail company preparing to migrate its data from an outdated, on-premises customer relationship management (CRM) system to Microsoft Dynamics 365 Business Central. The data set includes customer profiles, sales transactions, product information, and supplier data.

Tasks:

1. **Migration Planning:**

   - Outline a high-level migration plan that addresses the following:

     - Key objectives for the migration

     - Major risks that might be encountered and potential mitigation strategies

     - Resources needed for a successful migration (human, technological, time)

2. **Data Cleaning and Validation:**

- Develop a checklist for cleaning the company's customer data that includes

    - Steps to identify and correct inaccuracies in customer contact details

    - Techniques to deduplicate records

    - Validation processes to ensure the data conforms to the new system's requirements

3. **Data Security and Privacy:**

- Create a summary of actions to ensure the security and privacy of data during the migration, considering

    - Measures to protect sensitive customer data (like credit card information) during the transfer

    - How to comply with a relevant data protection law (e.g., GDPR if customers are in the EU)

    - Post-migration strategies to maintain data privacy in Business Central

Deliverables:

- A one-page migration plan outline

- A checklist for data cleaning of customer records

- A summary document detailing security and privacy actions

Upon completion of this exercise, you should have a practical understanding of the key steps and considerations in data migration and cleaning, as well as how to approach data security and privacy within the context of a Business Central implementation.

CHAPTER 6

Configuration and Customization

The process of adapting Microsoft Dynamics 365 Business Central to align with the unique needs of an organization entails a meticulous implementation and deliberate strategic planning. This chapter explores the essential elements of Business Central's adaptability, emphasizing the significance of configuration and modification to enhance the platform's impressive capabilities. This chapter offers a comprehensive guide for information technology professionals and business executives, presenting a systematic framework for integrating the features of Business Central into the daily activities of their company.

In conjunction with technical modifications, the comprehension and anticipation of business needs play a pivotal role in the setup and customization of Business Central. The purpose of this is to ensure that the software is compatible with the current operating framework and has the potential to scale in order to accommodate future expansion. This chapter aims to analyze the philosophical underpinnings that justify the importance of customization, the practical steps necessary to achieve a configuration that aligns with an organization's values, and the approaches for enhancing Business Central beyond its default functionalities through extensions.

© Dr. Gomathi S 2024
Dr. Gomathi S, *Mastering Microsoft Dynamics 365 Business Central*,
https://doi.org/10.1007/979-8-8688-0230-0_6

Management and Maintenance of Customizations

Customizing Microsoft Dynamics 365 Business Central is an ongoing process that extends beyond the initial setup and deployment. It's crucial to consider the management and maintenance aspects, especially in light of Microsoft's practice of releasing two major updates annually. These updates can significantly impact customizations, making it essential to have a proactive approach to maintenance.

Adapting to Major Releases

Microsoft's two major annual updates for Business Central can introduce changes that affect customizations. It's important to stay informed about these updates and test your customizations against them. This ensures that your customizations remain compatible and functional with the latest version of Business Central.

Utilizing Multiple Environments

Microsoft provides one production environment and three sandbox environments for Business Central. These sandbox environments are invaluable for safely developing, testing, and staging customizations before they are merged into the production environment. Best practices suggest using these environments as follows.

Development Environment

Use this for initial customization development and testing.

User Acceptance Testing (UAT) Environment

Before deploying to production, customizations should be thoroughly tested in a UAT environment that mirrors the production setup.

Staging Environment

This can be used for final testing post-UAT, especially for validating the integration of multiple customizations or complex changes.

Regular Review and Testing

Regularly review and test customizations, especially in anticipation of upcoming Microsoft releases. This helps in identifying and resolving any compatibility issues early.

Documentation and Training

Keep detailed documentation of all customizations and ensure that relevant staff are trained on any changes. This is crucial for both ongoing maintenance and for onboarding new team members.

Overview

The main objective of this chapter is to conduct a comprehensive analysis of the Configuration and Customization functionalities offered by Microsoft Dynamics 365 Business Central. You will possess the ability to acquire the necessary data to configure the system in a way that precisely reflects your business activities. This will guarantee that all operational divisions of your organization can engage in communication that is characterized by effectiveness and accuracy. Throughout this procedure, we shall assess the optimal protocols that safeguard the integrity of your system, while concurrently considering the unique characteristics of your business model.

Furthermore, we delve into the complexities associated with optimizing the operation of Business Central. By understanding and implementing extensions, an organization can overcome conventional limitations, fostering an environment of innovation and continuous improvement. The primary function of this chapter is to furnish individuals with not only technical guidance but also the knowledge necessary to make informed decisions that are consistent with their company's long-term objectives and operational needs.

Upon successful fulfillment of this chapter, readers will attain a comprehensive understanding of the strategies required to effectively configure and customize Business Central. This will enhance the seamless integration of technological advancements and operational protocols, ultimately resulting in favorable results.

Configuring Business Central for Business Process

Business Process

A business process refers to a cohesive set of interconnected actions or activities that, upon successful execution, lead to the achievement of a certain objective within an organization. These processes are essential components of a company's operations, since they establish a systematic and replicable approach to performing numerous functions, hence promoting efficiency, effectiveness, and adaptability.

One instance of a business process is the "Order to Cash" procedure. The process encompasses multiple stages that an enterprise undertakes, commencing with the receipt of an order from a customer and culminating in the acquisition of payment for said order. The following is an analysis of this procedure:

1. **Order Placement:** The process of order placement involves a customer initiating a purchase using several sales channels, including online platforms, in-person interactions, or telephonic communication.

2. **Order Processing:** Involves the systematic recording of order details inside a designated system, followed by a thorough verification of product or service availability.

3. **Credit Approval:** When dealing with new customers or significant orders, it might be imperative to perform a credit evaluation to determine the customer's capacity to meet payment obligations.

4. **Fulfillment:** The process by which a product is manufactured, assembled, or retrieved from inventory and prepared for distribution is referred to as fulfillment.

5. **Delivery:** The process through which the product is conveyed to the client or the service is rendered is referred to as "delivery."

6. **Invoicing:** Within the realm of business transactions, invoicing pertains to the procedure of transmitting a structured document to the client, delineating the precise sum due in exchange for the rendered goods or services.

7. **Payment Collection:** To obtain funds from consumers, the collection of payment is facilitated through a variety of channels, including bank transfers, Internet payments, and checks.

8. **Payment Recording and Reconciliation:** The payment recording and reconciliation procedure entails the documentation of payments within the financial system, followed by a verification of these payments against the corresponding invoices issued by customers.

In order for this procedure to be executed successfully, multiple organizational units—including sales, inventory management, transportation, accounting, and possibly customer service—must coordinate their efforts.

Configuring Business Central for Business Process

Ensuring the effective facilitation and enhancement of the company's operational activities through the enterprise resource planning (ERP) system is contingent upon the configuration of Business Central for business processes. The configuration of Business Central is crucial as it enables the system to accurately represent the distinctive characteristics of the organization, encompassing various aspects such as general ledger setup, customer relationship management, inventory management, and other relevant functionalities. An optimally structured system has the potential to enhance operational efficiency, minimize errors, and facilitate more informed decision-making.

The responsibility for configuring Microsoft Dynamics 365 Business Central is often a joint venture between the chosen vendor or partner organization and a dedicated team from the client's side. The vendor or partner, with their comprehensive understanding of Business Central's technical capabilities, plays a crucial role in tailoring the system. Concurrently, a team of key stakeholders from the client organization, typically comprising business analysts, system administrators, and department heads, brings in-depth knowledge of the organization's business goals and operational needs. This synergy between the vendor's technical expertise and the client team's organizational insight is essential. Together, they work diligently to ensure that the system's configuration is meticulously aligned with the organization's business processes and overarching objectives. This collaborative approach during the Discovery/ Requirement Gathering phase is fundamental to achieving a configuration that not only meets but enhances the organization's operational efficiency and goal attainment.

The selection of a configuration strategy is contingent upon the unique requirements and operational procedures of individual enterprises, therefore precluding the existence of a universally applicable approach. Nevertheless, a prevalent methodology entails the delineation of existing business processes, the identification of domains in which the enterprise resource planning (ERP) system might offer enhancements, and subsequently, the customization of the system to align with these processes. This may encompass the establishment of workflows, the delineation of data fields, and the customization of forms and reports.

Several important factors should be taken into consideration during the configuring process.

Gaining a comprehensive understanding of **the business requirements** for Business Central is of utmost importance. This entails engaging in communication with individuals across many departments within the organization in order to collect and ascertain the necessary specifications and demands.

Table 6-1. *Configuring Microsoft Dynamics 365 Business Central Across Various Business Domains*

Business Domain	Business Process	Example of Business Central Configuration
Sales	Lead to Order Process	The initial point of the Business Central Sales Module commences with Opportunities and Contacts. Within this module, we have the flexibility to incorporate various stages in the sales cycle. Additionally, at a fundamental level, we can document diverse activities, including meetings, calls, and more
Procurement	Vendor Management and Purchasing	Set up vendor profiles, automate purchase order creation based on inventory levels, and establish approval workflows for purchases
Inventory Management	Stock Replenishment	Configure inventory tracking, set automatic reorder points for stock, and link inventory levels to sales and purchase order systems
Finance and Accounting	Financial Reporting and Management	Implement general ledger setups, configure accounts receivable/payable, and set up financial reporting templates and consolidation rules
Manufacturing	Production Planning and Control	Set up production schedules, bill of materials, machine and labor capacity planning, and real-time production monitoring
Marketing	Campaign Development and Execution	Customize marketing modules for campaign planning, execution

(continued)

Table 6-1. (*continued*)

Business Domain	Business Process	Example of Business Central Configuration
Supply Chain	Logistics and Distribution Management	Set up supply chain modules for order fulfillment, shipping logistics, and tracking of goods in transit
Compliance	Regulatory Compliance Management	Set up audit trails, configure role-based access controls, and implement reporting tools for regulatory compliance like GDPR or SOX

Data integrity refers to the process of maintaining the consistency and accuracy of data entered into a system, with the aim of preserving the reliability and validity of reporting and analytics.

User Adoption: When configuring a system, it is crucial to take into account the user experience, ensuring that the system is designed in an intuitive manner and that appropriate training is offered to promote universal adoption.

Compliance and security considerations necessitate the configuration of the system to adhere to industry laws and safeguard sensitive data.

Iterative testing and feedback are key factors contributing to the achievement of successful configuration. This process entails the configuration of a certain component inside the system, followed by conducting tests with end users, collecting their input, and subsequently making necessary improvements prior to proceeding with the subsequent component of the system.

The utilization of an iterative method facilitates the establishment of a strong correlation between the system and the requirements of the business. Consequently, users are more inclined to embrace the system as they have actively participated in its development process.

The process of configuring Business Central for a business process include modifying the system in order to efficiently oversee and enhance the said operation. In this instance, we will consider the "Order to Cash" process as an illustrative example and examine the potential configuration of Business Central to facilitate its execution.

Sales order setup: The sales order setup involves the configuration of the sales order management module to effectively manage various sorts of orders. This may entail the implementation of automated order number sequencing, the specification of default payment terms, and the establishment of order processing procedures.

Inventory management involves the creation of item cards to represent products, which includes setting inventory levels, defining reordering policies, and establishing procedures for inventory monitoring and management. This functionality guarantees that the system possesses the capability to furnish up-to-date availability knowledge in real-time while a sales order is undergoing processing.

Credit control configuration involves the establishment of regulations regarding credit limits and the implementation of automated credit evaluations on client accounts in response to orders surpassing a pre-established threshold. This specific methodology enables the reduction of financial uncertainty and enhances the efficient management of accounts receivable.

Shipping and Delivery: To increase the efficacy of shipping and delivery operations, the configuration of the connection between the supply chain module and inventory management should be optimized. In order to improve the operational efficiency of the complete order fulfillment procedure—from order placement to successful product delivery—the successful execution of shipping agent operations, delivery time calculations, and sales order processing integration are critical components.

Invoicing: The integration of an automated procedure that generates invoices upon receipt of the dispatch confirmation constitutes the customization of the invoicing module. The system configuration ought to incorporate essential elements such as shipping expenses, tax obligations, promotional offers, and payment conditions.

Best Practice for Customization

Best practices for customization of an ERP system like Microsoft Dynamics 365 Business Central are essential to ensure that the system adds value without becoming overly complex or difficult to upgrade. Customization must be approached carefully to maintain system integrity, performance, and upgradability.

Why Customization Is Essential

Customization is essential because even with a robust system like Business Central, no out-of-the-box solution can meet every specific need of every business. Customization allows organizations to tailor the system to fit their unique processes, reporting requirements, and user experiences, thereby increasing efficiency, user adoption, and return on investment.

Who Is Responsible

The responsibility for customization typically falls upon a combined team of IT professionals, developers, system architects, and business analysts. They work together to understand the requirements, design the customizations, and implement them in a way that aligns with the business's needs while adhering to best practices.

Specific Techniques or Ways

- **Requirement Gathering and Analysis**: Conduct thorough needs analysis with stakeholders to understand what customizations are truly necessary.

- **Modular Approach**: Develop customizations in a modular fashion, so that they can be easily adjusted or removed if necessary.

- **Utilize Extensions**: In Business Central, prefer creating extensions over extending the core code. Extensions allow for easier system upgrades and maintenance.

- **Standard Coding Practices**: Adhere to standard coding practices and guidelines provided by Microsoft for Business Central.

Key Points to Consider

- **Assess Impact**: Before customizing, assess the impact on system performance, user experience, and future upgrades.

- **Prioritize Configurations**: Wherever possible, prefer system configurations over customizations to minimize complexity.

- **Scalability**: Ensure that customizations do not hinder the system's ability to grow with the business.

- **Documentation**: Maintain comprehensive documentation of all customizations for future reference and troubleshooting.

- **Testing**: Rigorous testing of customizations is essential to ensure they work as intended and do not introduce bugs or security vulnerabilities.

- **User Training**: Customizations are only as good as the users who utilize them. Proper training is essential to ensure that users understand how to use the new features effectively.

Secret to Reveal

A secret to effective customization is embracing the principle of "less is more." Start with the smallest change that will deliver the maximum benefit. This might involve using built-in tools for personalization before diving into code changes, such as adjusting user interfaces through personalization or creating custom report layouts.

Another hidden secret is to plan for the end at the beginning—consider how each customization will be affected by system updates or if a decision is made to revert to standard functionality. This foresight can save significant time and resources in the long run.

In conclusion, customization should be carefully balanced with the business needs, and best practices should be followed to ensure that Business Central remains a robust, scalable, and maintainable system that continues to deliver value throughout its lifecycle.

Extending Functionality with Extensions

In the dynamic world of enterprise resource planning (ERP), the ability to adapt and evolve with business needs is paramount. Microsoft Dynamics 365 Business Central provides a comprehensive framework for effectively overseeing a company's financial, operational, sales, and service aspects.

Nevertheless, the distinctiveness of every enterprise frequently requires a degree of customization that surpasses the conventional provision. Extensions are of paramount importance as they enhance and tailor the Business Central environment to suit the specific requirements of each enterprise. They provide a robust mechanism for enhancing functionality and tailoring it to specific needs.

Within the framework of Business Central, extensions provide the opportunity to incorporate novel functionalities or alter existing capabilities, all the while safeguarding the integrity of the ERP system's core architecture. This methodology not only ensures the integrity of the system and enhances the efficacy of the upgrading process, but also provides opportunities for advancements and adjustments. Extensions encompass a diverse array of enhancements, which may consist of simple modifications to the user interface or intricate modules that introduce novel functionalities. Ensuring the integrity of the fundamental system and preserving an integrated user experience are the primary objectives of this process.

By integrating extensions, organizations transition to a modular and adaptable enterprise resource planning (ERP) system, which enables them to effectively address evolving market requirements, regulatory landscapes, and internal process enhancements. As a result, the integration, implementation, and management of extensions have become a crucial element inside the Business Central ecosystem, providing businesses with a convenient means to continuously enhance their operations without causing any disruptions.

Best Practices for Using Extensions

Best practices for implementing extensions in Microsoft Dynamics 365 Business Central are critical for ensuring that customizations are efficient, manageable, and do not interfere with the basic functioning of the ERP system. Here's a thorough explanation of these excellent practices:

1. **Evaluate Existing Solutions Before Building New Ones:**

   - Before developing a new extension, it's crucial to explore existing solutions that might already address your needs. Microsoft AppSource is an excellent resource for finding a wide array of extensions and applications developed for Dynamics 365 Business Central. These solutions range from free to paid options and are often well-tested and supported by experienced vendors. By leveraging these pre-built solutions, you can avoid unnecessary development, ensuring that your customizations are both efficient and effective.

   - *Example:* Before creating a custom reporting tool, search Microsoft AppSource for reporting extensions that might already provide the advanced capabilities you need.

   - This approach ensures that the importance of Microsoft AppSource as a resource is clearly communicated within the context of evaluating existing solutions.

2. **Clearly Define Scope and Objectives:**

   - Have a clear understanding of what you want the extension to achieve. This helps to avoid scope creep and ensures that the extension serves a specific purpose without unnecessary features.

- *Example*: If the objective is to streamline the sales order process, the extension should be designed to optimize the steps involved in creating, approving, and fulfilling sales orders, and not extend into unrelated functionalities.

3. **Use AL Language and Visual Studio Code:**

   - Develop extensions using the AL language within Visual Studio Code, the recommended environment for Business Central development. This ensures compatibility and takes advantage of Microsoft's development tools.

   - *Example*: Utilizing snippets and IntelliSense in Visual Studio Code can speed up the development process and reduce errors.

4. **Build with Modularity in Mind:**

   - Create extensions that are modular, so they can be easily updated or replaced as business needs change without impacting other parts of the system.

   - *Example*: If you're extending the inventory management system, build it in a way that individual features, like stock level alerts, can be updated independently.

5. **Prioritize Performance:**

   - Ensure that your extensions do not negatively impact the performance of Business Central. This includes optimizing database interactions and avoiding unnecessary computations.

- *Example*: If the extension involves complex calculations, ensure they are performed efficiently, perhaps scheduled during off-peak hours.

6. **Focus on Upgradability:**

   - Design extensions so they do not hinder the upgrade path of Business Central. Avoid customizations that would conflict with new versions of the base application.

   - *Example*: Ensure that any integration points with Business Central's standard features are done using events and hooks that are less likely to be impacted by system upgrades.

7. **Rigorous Testing:**

   - Test extensions thoroughly in a development environment, including performance testing and user acceptance testing, before deploying them to production.

   - *Example*: Simulate a high-volume sales period to see how the new sales order extension performs under stress.

8. **Adhere to Security and Compliance Standards:**

   - Follow security best practices to protect sensitive data and ensure that the extension complies with relevant industry regulations.

   - *Example*: In order to process customer payment information, the extension must adhere to the PCI DSS requirements.

9. **Provide Comprehensive Documentation:**

   - Document the extension's capabilities, installation procedure, and any dependencies. This is essential for support and maintenance.

   - Produce a user document for the sales order extension that provides comprehensive instructions on utilizing its functionalities and resolving typical challenges.

10. **Ensure Seamless User Experience:**

    - Design the extension's user interface to be intuitive and consistent with the look and feel of Business Central to encourage user adoption.

    - *Example*: If adding new fields to a form, ensure they match the style and layout of existing fields.

11. **Plan for Ongoing Maintenance:**

    - Establish a strategy for extension maintenance that includes a timetable for routine updates and a method for monitoring and resolving problems. it's important to note that Microsoft releases two major updates for Business Central annually. Microsoft will notify us if there are any compatibility issues with our extensions and the planned new releases. Therefore, it is crucial to address and resolve all issues in our custom extensions before the updates are officially released by Microsoft.

    - As an example: Establish a quarterly evaluation procedure for the extension in order to rectify any concerns, implement enhancements, and revise documentation.

By adhering to these recommended approaches, enterprises can develop Business Central extensions that exhibit resilience, expandability, and enduring worth. Extensions ought to be perceived as dynamic constituents of the enterprise resource planning (ERP) system, undergoing development in tandem with the enterprises they facilitate.

Key Points to Consider

When expanding the capabilities of Microsoft Dynamics 365 Business Central, it is imperative to give due attention to a number of critical aspects in order to guarantee that the developed extensions deliver value and are in line with organizational goals.

1. **Business Need:**

    - Any extension should be motivated primarily by a clearly defined business requirement. This practice aids in concentrating the development endeavor and guarantees that the extension rectifies particular issues or enhances processes.

    - Explanation: Perform an exhaustive analysis of the fundamental company procedures and user requirements prior to development. This analysis ought to yield a concise declaration of the extension's intended purpose, thereby aiding in the prevention of feature growth and the addition of superfluous functionality that introduces complexity to the system.

2. **User Experience:**

- Extensions should be designed with the user experience at the forefront. They need to be intuitive, easy to use, and should integrate seamlessly into users' workflows.

- *Elaboration*: Consider the user journey within Business Central when using the extension. Simplify interactions, reduce the number of clicks to complete a task, and ensure that any new interfaces are consistent with the existing user interface of Business Central. Gathering user feedback during the design phase can greatly inform a user-centric design approach.

3. **Compatibility:**

- Assessing the extension's compatibility with both the current and future versions of Business Central is vital. It ensures that the extension remains functional and relevant as the platform evolves.

- *Elaboration*: Stay informed about the roadmap and updates for Business Central. Develop extensions using best practices and Microsoft's guidelines to mitigate the risk of future incompatibility. Use events and extensions rather than direct modifications to the core application to maintain compatibility with updates and upgrades.

4. **Maintenance:**

- Planning for ongoing maintenance is critical to the longevity and usefulness of the extension. Regular updates, bug fixes, and support will be required.

- *Elaboration*: Create a maintenance schedule that covers post-deployment monitoring, updates, and support for the extension. Set up a procedure for users to report problems and suggest improvements, and assign resources to the maintenance chores.

5. **Marketplace Potential:**

   - If the expansion solves a common need, it can have promise in the wider marketplace. Microsoft's AppSource might act as a platform to distribute the extension and establish an extra cash stream.

   - Discussion: Research the market to see if there is a demand for the capabilities provided by the extension. Prepare for the demanding standards and methods needed to list an extension on AppSource, including security, performance, and compliance tests.

Secret to Reveal

1. **Leveraging Community Feedback:**

   - The input from the community is a highly significant resource in the process of extension development. Interacting with the Business Central community offers valuable opportunities to gain insights into the requirements and challenges faced by users.

- Elaboration: Engage in active participation within forums, user groups, and other community platforms in order to get valuable feedback. Utilize this input to engage in an iterative process aimed at enhancing the design and functionality of the extension. The implementation of a collaborative method has the potential to greatly improve the applicability and ease of use of the extension.

2. **Embracing a "Fail Fast" Approach:**

- The notion of "fail fast" in extension development promotes the practice of swift prototyping and continuous improvement. This methodology facilitates expeditious discovery and resolution of concerns, so guaranteeing that the expansion aligns with user requirements without incurring superfluous time or expenses.

Elaboration: The proposed approach involves the implementation of an agile development process, characterized by the iterative development and testing of features within concise timeframes. This facilitates the timely identification of deficiencies and guarantees the progressive development of the extension through the incorporation of practical application and feedback. This approach mitigates the potential hazards associated with making substantial investments in a defective or misaligned product, while simultaneously fostering a culture that prioritizes ongoing enhancement.

Conclusion

This chapter highlights the importance of configuring and customizing Microsoft Dynamics 365 Business Central. It has emphasized the need for alignment with specific business processes, the delegation of responsibilities, and the adoption of best practices for customization. Additionally, we explored the role of extensions in enhancing system functionality.

As organizations rely on Business Central, mastering these techniques becomes essential for optimizing operational efficiency and future adaptability. With a focus on user experience, system integrity, and ongoing maintenance, businesses can leverage Business Central strategically.

This chapter serves as a foundation for comprehending Business Central configuration and customization, enabling organizations to remain competitive and agile in the evolving ERP landscape.

KEY HIGHLIGHTS

- Aligning Business Central with business processes for improved efficiency.

- Stakeholders like analysts and admins are responsible for configuration.

- Strategic customization is key for system integrity and future growth.

- Minimalistic customization for ease of upgrades and maintenance.

- Extensions add functionality without altering the core system.

- Ensuring compatibility with future updates when creating extensions.

- Designing with user experience and workflow efficiency in mind.

- Maintenance plans are essential for long-term customization viability.

- Customization can be domain-specific, such as in sales or inventory.

- Using community feedback and quick iteration enhances extension success.

CHAPTER 7

Change Management and User Adoption

Change management is the disciplined way of preparing and supporting individuals, teams, or even organizations in making organization change. It is an important building block to be incorporated for the success of that new technology, system, or ways of working in a sustainable way in that organization. This includes the ways that refocus or redefine the resources used, business processes, budget allocations, or any other operations means so as to reshape materially a company or organization.

Change management, in the context of Business Central implementation, represents the bridge between the technical solution given by the new system and on one side and the people who will use it on the other side. It stands for a smooth transition from old ways of working to new ones, minimizing the resistance and maximizing the engagement.

Meanwhile, user adoption is the process as to how the new solutions get implemented as current practices of the users. It is not learning how to work the new system, but it's about understanding and getting comfortable with the system being just another tool that can potentially help both the individual as well as the organization get what they're each hoping for. An effective user adoption strategy ensures the benefits of Business Central realized as the users embrace it in their normal day-to-day use.

© Dr. Gomathi S 2024
Dr. Gomathi S, *Mastering Microsoft Dynamics 365 Business Central,*
https://doi.org/10.1007/979-8-8688-0230-0_7

Overview

This chapter is dedicated to examining the pivotal role of change management in the effective roll-out of Business Central. We'll investigate the ways in which fostering an environment that is receptive to change can promote and hasten the embracement and operational success of the new system across your company. We will also detail robust training methods to make certain that every user is knowledgeable and at ease with Business Central, guaranteeing a smooth and enduring adoption. By the end of this section, you will have a clearer understanding of how to lead your team through transitions, tackle opposition, and achieve a unified shift to an improved workflow enabled by Business Central.

Importance of Change Transformation in Implementation

Change management is a cornerstone of successful implementation projects because it addresses the human element in organizational transformation. The importance of change management in the implementation of systems like Business Central cannot be overstated. It ensures that the technical solution provided by the software is fully utilized and effectively integrated into the business processes it aims to enhance or replace. By focusing on the people affected by the change, organizations can mitigate challenges that may arise from resistance to new processes and technologies.

In line with the significance of change management, it's crucial to establish clear goals and regularly evaluate the project's progress to gauge readiness. A notable approach in this context is Microsoft's "Success by Design" methodology. This framework is particularly effective across all Dynamics solutions, including Business Central. "Success by Design" emphasizes structured phases of implementation, starting from envisioning the project to its deployment and optimization. By adopting this method, organizations can benefit from a systematic and goal-oriented approach, ensuring that the technical solutions are not only implemented but also aligned with the business objectives. Moreover, this technique is readily accessible and can be adopted without additional costs, making it an efficient tool for organizations aiming to streamline their change management processes.

Who Is Responsible?

Responsibility for change management is typically multi-tiered. It involves

1. **Executive Leadership:** They are responsible for endorsing the change and setting the vision and expectations.

2. **Project Managers:** They oversee the implementation process, ensuring milestones are met and the project stays on track in terms of scope, quality, and timelines.

3. **Change Management Professionals:** They develop and execute the change management strategy, ensuring that the workforce is ready, willing, and able to perform their roles in the new environment.

4. **Human Resources:** They support the change on a personnel level, helping manage the impact on staff.

5. **Department Heads and Team Leaders:** They serve as advocates for change in their specific domains, offering assistance and direction to their team members.

6. **IT Department:** They guarantee a seamless implementation of the change's technical details and aid users throughout the transition period.

7. **Security and Permissions Team:** This team plays a crucial role in safeguarding the integrity of the new system. They are responsible for establishing and managing access controls, ensuring that only authorized personnel can access sensitive information.

Additionally, they oversee the process of isolating the older system to prevent any security breaches during the transition. Their involvement is vital to maintain the confidentiality, integrity, and availability of data throughout the change process.

Challenges and Pain Points

Change management encounters several obstacles and difficulties:

1. **Reluctance to Change:** Often the most substantial hurdle, employees might be resistant to new methodologies and systems due to unfamiliarity, insufficient understanding, or preference for current practices. Additionally, fear of failure can significantly contribute to this reluctance. Employees may worry about not being able to adapt to or perform well with the new system. Providing thorough training, practice sessions, and group support can help alleviate these fears.

2. **Communication Hurdles:** In the absence of consistent, transparent communication, the spread of inaccurate information can lead to confusion and opposition among staff. A significant barrier in this area can be language differences.
   Often, manuals and official documentation are available only in English, which can be challenging in a multilingual workforce. Ensuring that training and communication materials are available in the native language of the users can greatly enhance understanding and acceptance.

3. **Training Deficiencies:** Inadequate training may result in a lack of proficiency with new systems, impacting productivity and the rate at which users accept new procedures. Continuous support and opportunities for practice are essential to build confidence and competence in the new system.

4. **Disengagement:** If employees are not actively involved in the process of change, they may feel detached from the goals of the transformation, diminishing their willingness to embrace new methods.

5. **Ineffective Change Leadership:** Poor leadership during change can result in unclear direction, inadequate support, and a lack of responsibility, all crucial elements for the success of a change initiative. To overcome these challenges, a methodical change management approach is essential, encompassing strategic planning, communication, training, and support systems

that resonate with the organizational culture and objectives of the change. Properly addressing these aspects can alleviate the difficulties and support a more efficient transition to new systems and procedures.

6. **Increased Workload Challenges:** The introduction of a new system often coincides with the ongoing use of the current system, leading to an increased workload for users. This can result in a preference for committing to the current system over testing and familiarizing themselves with the new one. Balancing the demands of both systems is a critical challenge that needs to be managed carefully.

To overcome these challenges, a methodical change management approach is essential, encompassing strategic planning, communication, training, and support systems that resonate with the organizational culture and objectives of the change. Properly addressing these aspects can alleviate the difficulties and support a more efficient transition to new systems and procedures.

Creating a Positive Adoption Culture

The ADKAR model,[1] crafted by Prosci, is a methodology for managing change within organizations, emphasizing individual guidance through transitions. Its purpose is to confirm that change is not merely instituted but also welcomed by the impacted parties.

---

[1] www.prosci.com/methodology/adkar#:~:text=The%20word%20%E2%80% 9CADKAR%E2%80%9D%20is%20an,of%20more%20than%20700%20organizations

The components of the ADKAR model, complete with descriptions, instances, and their application to a Business Central deployment initiative, are outlined as follows:

1. **Awareness**

   - **Definition:** Understanding why change is necessary.

   - **Example:** Employees are made aware that the current legacy systems are costly and inefficient compared to the capabilities of Business Central.

   - **Business Central Application:** Communicate the benefits of Business Central over existing systems, such as real-time data access, improved reporting capabilities, and streamlined operations.

2. **Desire**

   - **Definition:** The willingness to support and engage in the change.

   - **Example:** Team members express a keen interest in learning the new system after understanding how it can make their day-to-day tasks easier.

   - **Business Central Application:** Hold sessions where key benefits tailored to each department are highlighted, demonstrating how Business Central will make individual jobs easier and contribute to career growth.

3. **Knowledge**

- **Definition:** Knowing how to change.

- **Example:** Providing training sessions on how to use Business Central's features.

- **Business Central Application:** Develop a comprehensive training program that covers all relevant Business Central functionalities for different roles within the organization.

4. **Ability**

- **Definition:** The capability to implement the change at the required performance levels.

- **Example:** Employees use Business Central in a test environment to carry out their regular tasks with support readily available.

- **Business Central Application:** Offer hands-on practice and support, possibly through a sandbox environment, where employees can safely explore and get used to the new system.

5. **Reinforcement**

- **Definition:** Ensuring that changes stay in place and that the transition is sustained.

- **Example:** Implementing a reward system for those who effectively use Business Central in their roles.

- **Business Central Application:** Recognize and reward departments or individuals who demonstrate proficient use of Business Central or who come up with innovative ways to use the system to improve business processes.

Sub-Techniques and Best Practices:

- For **Awareness**, use multiple communication channels like emails, workshops, and meetings to ensure the message reaches everyone.

- In fostering **Desire**, involve employees in the decision-making process where possible to increase buy-in.

- Regarding **Knowledge**, tailor training programs to different learning styles—some may benefit from hands-on workshops, while others may prefer self-paced online learning.

- To build **Ability**, pair users with change champions or super-users who can provide peer support.

- For **Reinforcement**, regularly solicit feedback and be prepared to address any issues or resistance that may threaten the sustainment of the change.

Using ADKAR for Business Central Projects:

- **Awareness:** Begin by sending out an organization-wide announcement about the switch to Business Central, explaining the limitations of the old system and how Business Central will benefit the company.

- **Desire:** Conduct an interactive session where you demonstrate how Business Central solves common pain points. Share success stories from other organizations that have benefited from its implementation.

- **Knowledge:** Organize training sessions segmented by departmental needs, ensuring that users understand the specific functionalities of Business Central that are relevant to their roles.

- **Ability:** Set up a pilot program where a select group from each department uses Business Central for their daily tasks, providing feedback and becoming proficient ahead of the full rollout.

- **Reinforcement:** After the implementation, hold regular check-ins, share success metrics of Business Central usage, and celebrate milestones to keep the team engaged and the new system's benefits top-of-mind.

By following the ADKAR model, organizations can structure their approach to implementing change, such as the introduction of Business Central, in a way that addresses the human side of change management and increases the chances of a successful and smooth transition.

Other Methodologies

There are several other methodologies and frameworks for managing the people side of change during an ERP implementation, including fostering a positive adoption culture. Here are a few:

1. **Kotter's 8-Step Change Model**[2]:

   - Create a sense of urgency.

   - Form a powerful coalition.

   - Create a vision for change.

   - Communicate the vision.

   - Remove obstacles.

---

[2] www.managementstudyguide.com/kotters-8-step-model-of-change.htm

- Create short-term wins.

- Build on the change.

- Anchor the changes in corporate culture.

Application: For Business Central, you could start by communicating the urgent need for more integrated and efficient systems. Form a coalition of leaders and influencers who champion the adoption of Business Central, and define what success looks like.

2. **Lewin's Change Management Model**[3]:

- Unfreeze: Prepare the organization for change by breaking down the existing status quo.

- Change: Execute the intended change.

- Refreeze: Ensure that the change is accepted and becomes the new norm.

Application: Use the "Unfreeze" phase to explain why Business Central is a necessary upgrade. During "Change," provide training and support. In "Refreeze," integrate Business Central into daily workflows and company culture.

3. **McKinsey's 7-S Model**[4]

- Strategy, Structure, Systems, Shared Values, Skills, Style, and Staff.

---

[3] www.mindtools.com/ajm9l1e/lewins-change-management-model
[4] https://corporatefinanceinstitute.com/resources/management/mckinsey-7s-model/

Application: Align Business Central's capabilities with the company's strategy, structure, and systems. Ensure that its adoption is consistent with the organization's shared values. Train staff to develop the necessary skills and adapt your management style to support the new system.

4. **Bridges' Transition Model**[5]:

- **Ending, Losing, and Letting Go**: People need to understand why the old way is no longer viable.

- **The Neutral Zone**: The phase between the old and the new, which can be used for creativity and getting buy-in.

- **The New Beginning**: People begin to embrace the new ways of working.

Application: Clearly communicate why the old ERP system is being replaced with Business Central. Use the transition period for training and encouraging innovation in how to use the new system. Celebrate the "New Beginning" when Business Central becomes the standard.

5. **Gartner's ADAPT Framework:**

- **Aspiration**: Set ambitious goals for the change.

- **Discovery**: Gather insights to inform the change strategy.

- **Architecture**: Design the change process.

- **People**: Enable people to drive the change.

- **Transformation**: Execute and sustain the change.

---

[5] https://wmbridges.com/about/what-is-transition/

Application: Set clear goals for Business Central implementation. Use discovery to understand how it can best serve your business needs. Design a tailored implementation plan. Empower your employees with the knowledge and skills to use Business Central effectively. Continuously monitor and refine the use of Business Central to achieve the transformation.

Each of these methodologies has different strengths and can be used in different combinations to suit the specific needs of an organization. Cultivating a culture that embraces adoption hinges on recognizing the specific dynamics within your organization and customizing the change management strategy to fit those needs.

With ERP systems such as Business Central, prioritizing transparent communication, extensive training, and continuous support is essential to facilitate a seamless shift and achieve strong user adoption rates.

Choosing the Right Methodology for Your Project

Selecting an appropriate change management approach for introducing Business Central requires evaluating factors such as the organizational culture, size, the complexity of the transition, and the implementation's objectives. Given the extensive nature of ERP systems like Business Central, blending multiple methodologies might provide the most comprehensive solution. Here is an analysis for comparison:

1. **ADKAR Model:**

   - **Pros**: Concentrates on personal change journeys; highly practical and centered on the user experience.

   - **Cons**: Might need to be complemented with wider organizational change management methods.

- **Suitability**: Exceptional for assuring individual readiness and capability to utilize Business Central efficiently, ideal for organizations that prioritize personal empowerment and responsibility.

2. **Kotter's 8-Step Change Model:**

- **Pros**: Outlines a strategic process for generating change momentum.

- **Cons**: Not as tailored to individual transitions, potentially requiring extra measures for user adoption.

- **Suitability**: Favored by organizations requiring a robust strategic structure, especially those experiencing major shifts with Business Central as a pivotal element.

3. **Lewin's Change Management Model:**

- **Pros**: Straightforward and digestible; underscores the need for solidifying new habits.

- **Cons**: May be overly simplistic and not reflect the complexities of continuous change.

- **Suitability**: Suitable for stable organizations where change is implemented incrementally.

4. **McKinsey's 7-S Model:**

- **Pros**: Addresses various organizational aspects to ensure thorough alignment.

- **Cons**: Complex execution and might lack clear directives for the human side of change.

- **Suitability**: Optimal for larger organizations that require harmonization across various departments for Business Central's successful induction.

5. **Bridges' Transition Model:**

   - **Pros**: Targets the emotional and psychological transitions of employees, critical for adoption.

   - **Cons**: Not as directive on the exact measures for managing change.

   - **Suitability**: Beneficial for organizations undergoing substantial cultural changes with the Business Central rollout.

6. **Gartner's ADAPT Framework:**

   - Pros: Encourages agility and innovation within the change management process.

   - Cons: May require a high maturity level in change management to execute effectively.

Suitability: Good for dynamic organizations that are used to change and innovation and are implementing Business Central in a fast-paced environment.

In conclusion, while ADKAR provides a solid foundation for ensuring individual readiness, combining it with a broader framework like Kotter's 8-Step Change Model could provide the strategic oversight and organizational momentum necessary for a successful Business Central implementation. The choice of methodology should ultimately align with the organization's change management maturity, culture, and the specific dynamics of the ERP implementation project.

Training Strategies for Users

The success of any enterprise resource planning (ERP) system like Business Central hinges not only on the software's capabilities but, crucially, on the ability and willingness of the users to adopt the system effectively. Training strategies are fundamental in bridging the gap between the potential of the software and the practical competence of the users. Here's why training strategies are vital:

- **Facilitate Smooth Transition:** Training prepares users for the transition from legacy systems or manual processes to Business Central, making the switch smoother and reducing resistance.

- **Enhance Productivity:** Well-trained users are able to leverage the system's capabilities to their full extent, which improves efficiency and productivity.

- **Reduce Errors:** Proper training minimizes the risk of errors that can occur when users are unfamiliar with the new system, saving time and cost in error correction.

- **Empower Users:** Training empowers users by providing them with the knowledge and skills to solve problems independently, reducing the dependency on a few experts.

- **Improve Adoption Rates:** Effective training is directly correlated with higher adoption rates, as users feel more confident and competent in using the new system.

- **Bolstering Change Management:** Education plays a crucial role in change management efforts, equipping users with an understanding of the change's purpose and the know-how to manage it effectively.

- **Customization and Applicability:** Personalized training sessions help users grasp how Business Central integrates with their individual responsibilities and daily activities, enhancing the training's impact and retention.

- **Securing Return on Investment (ROI):** Optimal use of Business Central's functionalities and tools, achieved through dedicated training, is key to realizing the system's full ROI.

User training strategies are a vital element in the successful uptake of systems like Business Central. Quality training significantly boosts user skill and assurance, which translates into heightened efficiency and better exploitation of the system's capabilities. Here are some tactics to contemplate:

1. **Role-Based Training:**

   - Tailor training sessions to the specific roles and responsibilities of users.

   - Focus on the features and processes that each role will use most frequently.

2. **Blended Learning:**

   - Combine various training methods, such as in-person sessions, online courses, webinars, and self-paced learning modules.

   - Accommodate different learning styles and schedules.

3. **Hands-On Practice:**

   - Provide users with access to a training environment where they can practice without affecting live data.

   - Encourage learning by doing, which can improve retention.

4. **Just-In-Time Training:**

   - Offer training materials and resources available on-demand when users need them.

   - Use helpdesk support, FAQs, and in-application assistance.

5. **Train the Trainer:**

   - Train a select group of users who can then support their colleagues.

   - These "super users" or "change champions" can provide peer-to-peer training and assistance.

6. **Gamification:**

   - Introduce elements of play, competition, and rewards into the training process.

   - Use quizzes, badges, and leaderboards to motivate users.

7. **Continuous Learning:**

   - Recognize that training is not a one-time event but an ongoing process.

   - Offer refresher courses and advanced training as users become more comfortable with the basics.

8. **Feedback and Adaptation:**

- Collect feedback on the training programs to identify what is working and what is not.

- Be prepared to adapt the training approach based on this feedback.

9. **Mentoring and Support Networks:**

- Establish a system where users can seek help from more experienced colleagues.

- Create forums or chat groups for users to share tips and solutions.

10. **Documentation and Resource Libraries:**

- Provide comprehensive user guides, how-to documents, and best practices manuals.

- Ensure that documentation is easily accessible and kept up to date.

11. **Real-World Scenarios and Case Studies:**

- Use examples and case studies that are relevant to the users' real work situations.

- Encourage users to apply what they learn to their own job tasks.

12. **Phased Training Approach:**

- Break the training into phases, starting with core functionalities and gradually moving to more advanced features.

- This can help prevent information overload.

For Business Central specifically, it's important to focus training on the areas that will be used daily by the various roles within the organization. For instance, accounting personnel should receive in-depth training on financial modules, while warehouse staff should be trained on inventory management and Warehouse Management (bins, Pic, Petaway, warehouse receipts, etc.) features. Training should also cover any customizations or integrations that are specific to the organization's implementation of Business Central.

Type of Training

The type of training provided for Business Central or any ERP system should be multifaceted to address different roles, skill levels, and learning preferences.[6] Here are the types of training that can be considered:

1. **Onboarding Training:**

   - Introduces new users to Business Central basics

   - Covers fundamental navigation and core modules

2. **Role-Specific Training:**

   - Customized to the needs and daily tasks of specific roles within the organization

   - Focuses on the functionality each role will use, such as sales processing for sales teams or financial reporting for accounting

---

[6] https://in.indeed.com/career-advice/career-development/
methods-of-training

3. **Modular Training:**

   - Breaks down training into modules based on Business Central's features, like inventory management, financials, or customer relationship management (CRM)

   - Allows users to learn about features relevant to their work area in manageable parts

4. **Instructor-Led Training (ILT):**

   - Conducted by a trainer in real-time, either in person or via virtual classrooms

   - Encourages interaction and immediate feedback

5. **E-Learning:**

   - Online courses that can be self-paced and accessed anytime, anywhere

   - Can include a mix of text, video, quizzes, and interactive content

6. **Hands-On Workshops:**

   - Interactive sessions where users can practice tasks in a controlled environment

   - Facilitates experiential learning and retention

7. **Webinars and Live Demos:**

   - Scheduled online sessions focusing on specific topics or updates

   - Can be recorded for later viewing

8. **Support and Coaching:**

- One-on-one support or small group coaching sessions for personalized assistance

- Helps users who need extra attention or have specific questions

9. **Knowledge Base and Documentation:**

- Written guides, how-to articles, FAQs, and best practice documents.

- Users can reference these materials as needed for self-help.

10. **Video Tutorials and Screencasts:**

- Recorded video guides that demonstrate processes step-by-step

- Beneficial for visual learners and for conveying complex procedures

11. **Peer Training:**

- Having more experienced users or "super users" train their peers

- Encourages knowledge sharing and team collaboration

12. **Certification Programs:**

- Offer certifications for different levels of proficiency

- Motivate users to reach a certain level of competency

13. **Gamified Learning:**

- Incorporating game design elements in training to make learning more engaging

- Can include points, badges, leaderboards, and rewards

14. **Just-In-Time Training:**

- Providing training materials at the moment they are needed, such as quick help guides or context-sensitive help within Business Central

15. **Training via Simulation:**

- Using simulated environments to train users on Business Central without the risk of affecting live data

16. **Continuous Professional Development:**

- Ongoing training sessions to cover new features, updates, or deeper dives into existing functionality

The type of training chosen should align with the organization's culture, the complexity of the implementation, the users' proficiency levels, and the resources available. A blend of these training types often results in the most comprehensive and effective training program.

Summary

In conclusion, the journey through Change Management and User Adoption is an integral part of a successful Business Central implementation. Recognizing the critical role of change management helps in anticipating and mitigating resistance, thereby facilitating a smoother transition. By employing models such as ADKAR, Kotter's

8-Step Change Model, or any other effective change management strategy, businesses can navigate the complexities of organizational change with greater ease and support.

Creating a positive adoption culture is not incidental; it is crafted through deliberate and strategic efforts that encompass leadership commitment, comprehensive communication, and inclusive involvement. The culture thrives on a shared vision and is sustained by continuous reinforcement and the demonstration of tangible benefits from the new system.

Training strategies act as the scaffold for this transformation, enabling users to not only familiarize themselves with Business Central but to master it, thereby unlocking the system's full potential. From role-specific training to interactive e-learning, the methods employed must cater to diverse learning styles and preferences, ensuring every user is confident and competent in utilizing the system.

This chapter underscores the importance of a well-thought-out approach to managing the human aspects of the Business Central implementation. Ultimately, the goal is to ensure that the organization not only adopts the new system but also embraces it as a catalyst for business efficiency, growth, and competitive advantage. The success of the implementation is reflected not just in a new system going live, but in the thriving productivity and innovation that comes from people using the system to its fullest potential.

CHAPTER 8

Integration with Existing Systems

In the dynamic landscape of modern business, the ability to seamlessly integrate both existing and upcoming systems is crucial. As organizations grow and evolve, introducing new technologies like Business Central alongside existing or newly added systems such as Point of Sales solutions or new eCommerce platforms becomes integral to their progression. This chapter addresses the intricacies of integrating diverse systems, offering a systematic approach to achieving efficient synergy between Business Central and other systems, whether they are long-standing or newly adopted.

The integration process involves understanding technical requirements, identifying effective connection points, and implementing solutions that synchronize data across platforms with minimal disruption to ongoing operations. This balance between established and new systems is vital, ensuring Business Central's implementation enhances value without creating operational conflicts.

Key Stakeholders and Project Dynamics

Recognizing the "Other System Vendor" as a key stakeholder is essential. Whether integrating existing or new systems, adjustments in terms of APIs or other methods are typically required by the respective vendors. The Business

Dr. Gomathi S, *Mastering Microsoft Dynamics 365 Business Central*,
https://doi.org/10.1007/979-8-8688-0230-0_8

Central team relies on these vendors, especially in cases of integrating external solutions like a Warehouse Management System (WMS) developed by a third party.

Often, Business Central projects and integration projects run in parallel, which is a significant project consideration. Delays by an "Other System Vendor" can profoundly impact the overall integration timeline and success. This interdependency highlights the importance of effective project management and clear communication between all parties involved.

Addressing Integration Challenges

A notable challenge in integrations is the occurrence of "Quarantined Transactions"—transactions that fail to transfer between systems due to reference or master data issues. Regular involvement and problem-solving by the IT department and end-user departments are crucial to ensure these transactions are resolved and reach their intended destinations.

System Integration Testing (SIT) and User Acceptance Testing (UAT)

A critical phase in the integration process is the "Systems Integration Test" (SIT), where both vendors test the integration for integrity, performance, and adherence to specifications. Following a successful SIT, the "User Acceptance Test" (UAT) is conducted, involving both vendors and the end-user teams. This phase is crucial for verifying that the integration meets user requirements and functions as intended in a real-world environment.

Utilizing Microsoft AppSource for Integration

Microsoft AppSource is a significant resource for application integrations, offering a variety of solutions with standard connectors that simplify the integration process. Platforms like Shopify and Salesforce provide ready-to-deploy integrations available on Microsoft AppSource, reducing the need for extensive development work. For more information, visit Microsoft AppSource.

Considering Performance and Throughput

Performance or throughput, defined as the maximum number of transactions per minute or hour, is a vital aspect of integration discussions. Both system vendors must ensure the integration can handle peak demands, such as during Christmas shopping for eCommerce sites or month-end processing for banking systems. These requirements must also account for anticipated future growth in transaction volumes, safeguarding the scalability and longevity of the integration solution.

Overview

This chapter goes deeply into the strategic planning and execution stages involved in integrating Dynamics 365 Business Central from Microsoft with an organization's existing systems. This book has been designed to furnish you with a comprehensive comprehension of the procedures and optimal strategies associated with establishing a unified ecosystem in which Business Central not only complements but also coexists with the preexisting technological infrastructure.

This chapter will delve into the fundamental elements of integration, beginning with the initial phase of comprehending the requirements of your organization and progressing to the intricate technical details involved in attaining automation and real-time data synchronization. Upon completion of this chapter, readers will possess the requisite understanding to approach integration with assurance, thereby guaranteeing that their investment in Business Central produces the utmost return through the improvement of operational efficiency and decision-making capabilities.

Understanding Integration Requirements

Grasping the integration requirements is crucial for ensuring that Business Central's deployment aligns with the organization's objectives and existing infrastructure. This task, demanding a blend of technical know-how and business process insight, typically involves the collaboration of functional consultants, technical consultants, and a key stakeholder: the vendor of the existing systems to be integrated.

Functional consultants are at the forefront in gathering and defining the business requirements. They work closely with critical stakeholders, including the in-house IT team that may have developed existing systems, to understand essential aspects like data usage, workflows, and business processes vital for the organization's management. Their expertise lies in identifying the requirements that the software must meet and translating these into functional specifications.

Technical consultants, on the other hand, take these functional requirements and evaluate their technical feasibility. Their role extends to the actual integration process, encompassing data migration, system configurations, and customizations. They need to comprehend Business Central's capabilities and limitations and the technical aspects of its integration with other systems. Here, the involvement of the vendors of the existing systems becomes indispensable. These vendors, possessing intimate knowledge about the integration capabilities of their systems, play a crucial role in preparing these systems for integration. Their insights and cooperation are vital to ensure that the integration is not only technically feasible but also aligns with the functional and operational needs of the organization.

Simple Scenario

Imagine a company that uses an old CRM system and is now implementing Business Central to streamline its operations. The functional consultant would begin by understanding how the sales team uses the CRM, what data they capture, how this data feeds into the sales process, and what outputs or reports they require.

For instance, the sales team might need to ensure that customer contact details from the CRM are available in Business Central to generate quotes and invoices efficiently. The functional consultant would document these needs and any specific workflows that the integration must support.

With the gathered information, the technical consultant's next step is to strategize the integration of the CRM system with Business Central. This involves a collaborative effort with at least three key stakeholders: the CRM vendor, the middleware vendor (if middleware is used), and the end users. The consultant coordinates with the CRM vendor to understand the system's capabilities and requirements for integration. If a middleware platform is necessary for facilitating data exchange, the middleware vendor's expertise becomes crucial to ensure seamless connectivity and data flow. The consultant also plans the data migration process, working closely with these vendors and the users to guarantee that customer contact details are consistently synchronized between the two systems. The aim is to establish an API or middleware solution that enables real-time data exchange, reflecting updates across both systems promptly and accurately.

In this scenario, both consultants play vital roles. The functional consultant ensures that the integration meets the business's needs, while the technical consultant makes it happen in a practical and efficient manner. Collaboration between the two ensures that the integrated system is both functional and technically sound.

The Role of Functional Consultants in Collecting Integration Requirements

Functional consultants play a pivotal role in gathering integration requirements. They act as a bridge between the business's operational needs and the technical capabilities of new systems like Business Central. Their main task is to ensure that the software implementation will fulfill the business requirements and support the company's processes effectively.

Who Do They Collect Requirements From?

Functional consultants gather requirements from various stakeholders within the organization, each playing a crucial role in the integration process. These stakeholders typically include

- **Business Leaders and Executives:** Their input is vital to understand the strategic objectives and how the integration can support these goals, ensuring alignment with the company's broader vision.

- **End Users:** Engaging with end users provides insights into daily workflows and the practical needs from the new system, helping to ensure that the integration enhances user experience and efficiency.

- **IT Department:** To gain insight into the existing technical infrastructure, constraints, and crucially, the security requirements. This includes understanding how the integration will adhere to the company's cybersecurity policies and data protection standards, ensuring the safe and secure handling of data across systems.

- **Data Analysts:** They play a key role in identifying the types of data that need to be synchronized and understanding how these data are currently used, contributing to effective data management strategies.

- **Vendor of the Other System:** It is crucial to include the vendor of the system that Business Central will be integrated with. Their knowledge and cooperation are essential for a smooth integration process, as they provide insights into the capabilities, limitations, and best practices for their system.

Scenario and Example

Consider a retail company aiming to integrate Business Central with its online eCommerce platform. Initially, the functional consultant engages with the eCommerce team to gain a comprehensive understanding of their management of online orders, inventory, customer data, and payment processes. Discussions with the finance department are also crucial to determine the integration of sales data into Business Central's financial reporting.

Further, this integration opens up more advanced possibilities, such as real-time inventory availability and dynamic pricing information being accessible on the eCommerce portal. The sales team plays a vital role in this scenario, contributing their insights on these new features that enhance customer experience and operational efficiency.

Key stakeholders in this integration project include the Sales and Finance teams, the eCommerce and Business Central vendors, and the IT Department. The latter ensures that the integration aligns with security protocols and infrastructural capabilities, making it a comprehensive effort that leverages the strengths of each department and technology.

For example, in the case of an eCommerce platform integration, the functional consultant plays a crucial role in ensuring that online sales patterns of customers are effectively captured and reflected in Business Central. This involves mapping and translating the data related to customer purchasing behavior and trends from the eCommerce platform to Business Central. This integration is key to gaining valuable insights into customer preferences and buying habits, which can then be used to enhance sales strategies and inventory management within Business Central.

The phases can be conveniently remembered with the acronym "DREAM," which stands for Discovery, Requirements, Evaluation, Alignment, and Mapping.

1. **Discovery (D)**: This initial phase involves the functional consultant conducting interviews and meetings with stakeholders to gather information on the business's processes, systems, and challenges. They observe the current workflow, document existing system functionalities, and identify the touchpoints where integration with Business Central is needed. This is also when they establish the scope of the integration.

2. **Requirements (R)**: After understanding the business workflow, the functional consultant outlines the specific requirements. This includes what data needs to be integrated, the direction of data flow, the frequency of data updates,

and any specific business rules that need to be applied during the integration. They also pinpoint the targeted results and the ways in which the integration will bolster business aims.

3. **Evaluation (E)**: During this stage, the functional consultant appraises Business Central's technical prowess in relation to the specified needs. Comprehending the technical scope and limitations is essential to confirm that business requirements are achievable. This typically necessitates a joint effort with technical consultants to gauge the practicability and to pinpoint the required customizations or settings.

4. **Alignment (A)**: With the demands identified and assessed, the functional consultant ensures they are in sync with Business Central's features. They see to it that the needs are sorted based on priority and congruence with business objectives, and they concoct a comprehensive plan for integration. Part of this phase is defining the roles and responsibilities of everyone involved and establishing clear integration expectations.

5. **Mapping(M)**: In this concluding phase, the functional consultant delineates the data fields and processes that will be consolidated. They compile exhaustive documentation detailing the data migration process, including any necessary data conversions or checks. This blueprint is vital for the technical crew to accurately set up the integration.

Throughout these phases, the functional consultant must maintain clear and constant communication with both the business stakeholders and the technical team. They act as a bridge between the business needs and the technical implementation, ensuring that the integration supports the business processes and adds value to the organization.

DREAM Phases Detailed with Example and Methods:

1. **Discovery (D):**

   - **Example:** A functional consultant is working with a manufacturing company that wants to integrate Business Central with its legacy production tracking system.

   - **Method:** The consultant conducts on-site observations and interviews with production managers, IT staff, and floor operators. They document the current workflow of production data, understand the pain points such as delays in updating inventory levels, and pinpoint where real-time data integration with Business Central could alleviate these issues.

   - **Outcome:** They establish the scope of integration, such as real-time updating of inventory levels in Business Central as products are completed on the production floor.

2. **Requirements (R):**

   - **Example:** The same manufacturing company needs to ensure that the production data is accurately reflected in Business Central for inventory management and financial reporting.

- **Method:** The consultant determines what specific data (e.g., production counts, machine usage stats) needs to be synchronized between the systems. They define the direction of data flow (from the production tracking system to Business Central), establish how often data should be updated (e.g., every hour), and outline any business rules (like data validation checks before synchronization).

- **Outcome:** A requirements document is created that details these needs and expected outcomes like improved inventory accuracy and timely financial reporting.

3. **Evaluation (E):**

   - **Example:** The company's legacy system is quite dated, and there is a concern about its compatibility with Business Central.

   - **Method:** The functional consultant evaluates the technical capabilities of both systems, often using tools such as Business Central's APIs documentation and the legacy system's technical manuals. They collaborate with technical consultants to assess whether existing interfaces can support the needed integration or if new middleware is required.

   - **Outcome:** A feasibility report that states what can be directly integrated, what requires customization, and what might need third-party solutions to bridge any gaps.

4. **Alignment (A):**

- **Example:** Priorities may conflict; for instance, finance requires real-time data for reporting, but the production team is concerned about system performance.

- **Method:** The functional consultant facilitates discussions between departments to prioritize requirements. They then align these priorities with the capabilities of Business Central, adjusting the project scope if necessary. They develop a project plan, which includes milestones, roles, and responsibilities.

- **Outcome:** A document for project coordination that specifies the order of integration priorities, the timetable for milestones in the project, and the agreement on the project's objectives.

5. **Mapping (M):**

- **Example:** The mapping between data fields in the production monitoring system and their corresponding fields in Business Central is required.

- **Method:** The functional consultant aligns data fields among the two systems utilizing spreadsheets or data mapping tools. They specify the transformation, validation, and synchronization of each field. To ensure data integrity, this may entail the development of rules for transformation for data formats or the implementation of validation procedures.

- **Outcome:** A comprehensive data mapping guide that serves as a blueprint for the technical team to configure the integration. This includes field-by-field instructions and any necessary transformation logic.

By adhering to the DREAM methodology, a functional consultant ensures a structured and thorough approach to integrating Business Central with existing systems, minimizing risks and aligning the integration with the company's business objectives.

Technical Consultants' Role in Collecting Integration Requirements

Technical consultants specialize in the technological aspects of system integrations, focusing on how different software can be interconnected, how data can be transferred efficiently and securely, and how systems can be configured to operate together seamlessly. Their role is to translate the business needs and functional requirements into technical specifications that can be implemented by developers and IT professionals.

Whom They Interact With

Technical consultants typically gather requirements from

- **Functional Consultants:** To understand the business needs and functional requirements that the technical solutions must fulfill.

- **IT Staff and System Administrators:** To comprehend the current technical infrastructure and its capabilities.

- **Data Security Teams:** To ensure the integration complies with security standards and data protection regulations.

- **End Users or Department Heads:** Occasionally, to understand how the integration will impact their daily work and to gather specific technical needs or preferences.

Scenario and Example

Let's consider a logistics company that wants to integrate Business Central with its warehouse management system (WMS). The functional consultants have determined that real-time inventory levels and shipping information need to be shared between the two systems.

The technical consultant would need to

1. Evaluate the current WMS's API capabilities or other integration techniques and data structure.

2. Determine how to establish a secure and reliable data exchange between the systems.

3. Assess if the WMS can handle the additional load of frequent updates from Business Central.

4. Develop a technical plan that includes how the systems will communicate, any necessary middleware, and data transformation protocols.

Phases of Technical Requirement Collection

The process can be segmented into five key phases, which can be remembered by the acronym "STEAM":

1. **System Analysis (S):**

    - In this phase, the technical consultant collaborates closely with the vendor of the existing system, such as the Warehouse Management System (WMS) in this context, to thoroughly assess the technical landscape. This joint analysis includes reviewing software versions, hardware specifications, and network configurations of the existing system. Together, they identify any technical limitations and explore opportunities for integration with Business Central.

    - This collaborative approach ensures that the technical consultant gains a comprehensive understanding of the system's capabilities and constraints, which is essential for planning a successful integration strategy.

2. **Technical Requirement Gathering (T):**

    - This involves translating the functional requirements into technical specifications.

    - They determine what technologies will be used for the integration, such as REST APIs, web services, or data import/export tools.

3. **Evaluation of Integration Methods (E):**

    - The consultant evaluates different methods and tools for integration.

    - They might consider using direct API connections, middleware, or even a custom-built solution.

4. **Alignment with Technical Capabilities (A):**

    - This phase ensures that the technical requirements align with the system's capabilities and business objectives.

    - It often involves back-and-forth discussions with functional consultants and IT staff to refine the technical approach.

5. **Mapping and Prototyping (M):**

    - The technical consultant maps out the data flow between systems and develops prototypes.

    - They create detailed documentation for developers on how the integration should be implemented.

In-Depth Look at the Phases:

- **S:** The technical consultant performs a technical discovery, understanding the capabilities and constraints of the current system and how they can be augmented to support the integration.

- **T:** They gather all technical details that will influence the integration, such as data formats, volume, frequency of updates, security requirements, and any specific technical needs from different departments.

- **E:** Different integration methods are evaluated for feasibility, security, efficiency, and cost. This could involve researching third-party integration tools or the development of custom solutions.

- **A:** The consultant ensures that the technical plan aligns with the business goals identified by the functional consultants and the technical capabilities identified in the System Analysis phase.

- **M:** Here, they define exactly how data will be mapped from one system to another, what transformations or data processing steps are required, and they may develop a prototype to demonstrate and test the integration concept.

Throughout these phases, the technical consultant's role is crucial to designing a technically sound integration strategy that meets business requirements and leverages the full capabilities of Business Central. They ensure that the technical aspects of the integration are feasible, secure, and optimized for performance.

Table 8-1. *Comparing the Roles of Functional and Technical Consultants in Integration Requirement Collection*

Aspect	Functional Consultant	Technical Consultant
Primary Focus	Business processes, workflows, and requirements gathering	System capabilities, technical feasibility, and implementation specifics
Key Responsibilities	Understanding business needs, translating them into system requirements, ensuring alignment with business goals	Evaluating technical solutions, ensuring security and compliance, developing technical specifications
Interactions	Business leaders, end users, IT department, data analysts	Functional consultants, system administrators, security teams, occasionally end users
Example	Identifying the need for real-time inventory updates in Business Central when sales occur on an eCommerce platform	Assessing whether Business Central's APIs can support the necessary data exchanges with an eCommerce platform
Outcome	A detailed requirements document outlining how the integration should support business processes	Technical specifications and a prototype demonstrating the integration between Business Central and the eCommerce platform

Integrating Business Central with Other Tools

Business Central's robust capability to integrate with other tools is one of its most powerful features, allowing businesses to streamline operations, enhance productivity, and ensure a unified platform as shown in Figure 8-1 for various business functions.

1. **Power Automate**: Power Automate is a service that helps create automated workflows between your favorite apps and services to synchronize files, get notifications, collect data, and more. When integrated with Dynamics 365 Business Central, Power Automate can be used to create workflows that automate tasks across different applications. For instance, a workflow could be set up to automatically create a new contact in Dynamics 365 whenever a new lead is added in Salesforce, or to post a message on a Twitter account whenever a marketing campaign is launched in Dynamics 365.[1]

---

[1] https://powerautomate.microsoft.com/en-in/

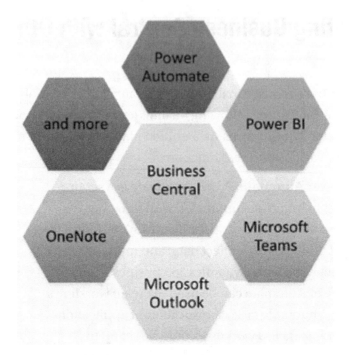

Figure 8-1. *Business Central Integration with other tools*

2. **Power BI**: This Microsoft business analytics tool offers dynamic visualizations and intelligence capabilities, enabling users to craft reports and dashboards. Its fusion with Dynamics 365 enables immediate data scrutiny and the distribution of insights within the enterprise. Users can tailor dashboards to harness Dynamics 365 data for real-time business tracking and analytical insights.[2]

---

[2]www.microsoft.com/en-us/power-platform/products/power-bi

3. **Microsoft Teams**: As a platform for communication and collaboration, Teams integrates workplace chat, video meetings, and file storage. Its Dynamics 365 integration lets users pull up customer data during Teams interactions, enhancing collaboration through direct discussions about customer needs and opportunity management, all within a single application.[3]

4. **Microsoft Outlook**: Microsoft Outlook's integration with Business Central enhances communication efficiency by enabling the direct logging of emails into customer records within Dynamics 365. This streamlined process allows users to easily create new Dynamics 365 entries directly from their email inbox. Additionally, Business Central's comprehensive email integration permits actions such as sending quotations directly from Business Central using Outlook. Users can also access detailed customer and vendor insights directly within Outlook, providing a centralized view of communication histories and essential contact information.

5. **OneNote**: Linking OneNote with Dynamics 365 organizes notes and information like meeting recaps related to Dynamics 365 records, ensuring that data is consolidated and readily available to the team.[4]

---

[3] www.microsoft.com/en-in/microsoft-teams/group-chat-software

[4] www.microsoft.com/en-in/microsoft-365/onenote/digital-note-taking-app

6. **Office 365 (Now Microsoft 365)**: Integrating Microsoft 365 with Dynamics 365 unites productivity tools such as Outlook, Word, Excel, and OneNote, allowing for document creation, email tracking, appointment scheduling, and note-taking within Dynamics 365.[5]

7. **Microsoft Exchange**: Synchronizing Exchange with Dynamics 365 keeps contacts, appointments, and interactions aligned, proving particularly beneficial for sales and service teams by integrating emails and calendar events from Exchange into Dynamics 365 for improved scheduling and client communication tracking.[6]

These integrations amplify Dynamics 365's efficiency, turning it into a holistic business management system. Successful integration is about tailoring to your organization's needs, automating workflows, and configuring settings to fully leverage the integration's potential.

Data Synchronization and Automation in Business Central

Data coordination and automation play vital roles in the smooth functioning of business systems. They maintain uniformity of data across various platforms and manage repetitive actions autonomously, boosting efficiency and minimizing the chances of mistakes.

---

[5] www.microsoft.com/en-in/microsoft-365

[6] www.microsoft.com/en-in/microsoft-365/exchange/email

Data Synchronization

Data synchronization involves creating and maintaining data consistency between a source and a target storage, and continuously aligning this data over time. Within the framework of Business Central, this synchronization ensures that data within Business Central and connected systems—such as CRM, eCommerce, or supply chain management tools—remains current and accurate.

For example, when a sale occurs on an eCommerce platform, it's crucial that the inventory levels in Business Central are updated promptly. Failing to synchronize in real-time could result in selling more items than available, leading to customer dissatisfaction.

Thus, synchronization is more than just data replication; it's about preserving data integrity and uniformity across an organization's entire suite of business applications.

Automation

In Business Central, automation signifies the development of self-sufficient processes capable of executing tasks independently, without the need for human input. Automation can be applied to a wide array of repetitive tasks such as data entry, invoice generation, report creation, or even complex workflow processes.

For example, Business Central can be set up to automatically generate purchase orders when inventory levels fall below a certain threshold. This automation would involve monitoring inventory levels, determining when reordering is necessary, and then creating and sending purchase orders to the appropriate vendors—all without manual input.

How It Works Together

The combination of data synchronization and automation can significantly boost operational efficiency. Consider a scenario where a company uses Business Central integrated with their customer service platform:

- **Data Synchronization:** When a customer service representative updates a customer's address in the service platform, that change is immediately reflected in Business Central due to real-time data synchronization. This ensures that the billing department always has the most current information when they generate invoices.

- **Automation:** Along with the updated address, an automated workflow could trigger a confirmation email to the customer, ensuring they are aware of the change in their records. Furthermore, if the customer's update indicates a new geographic market, Business Central could automatically adjust tax rates or shipping costs associated with the customer's orders.

Phases of Implementation

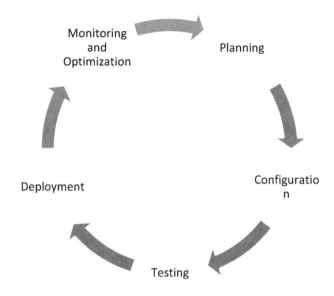

Figure 8-2. *Implementation phase cycle*

1. **Planning:** Identifying which data needs to be synchronized and what business processes can be automated.

2. **Configuration:** Establishing the protocols for data synchronization and the pathways for automated processes within Business Central and associated systems.

3. **Testing:** Executing rigorous assessments to confirm the effectiveness of the synchronization and automated systems, ensuring there is no data loss or redundancy.

4. **Deployment:** Applying the established data synchronization and automated procedures into the operational environment.

5. **Monitoring and Optimization:** Consistently reviewing the implemented systems to guarantee their optimal performance and conducting necessary enhancements.

Through the successful deployment of data synchronization and automation, companies can alleviate the burden of manual tasks, diminish the potential for errors caused by manual handling, and maintain confidence that their data-centric decisions are informed by the most up-to-date and precise data obtainable.

Conclusion

In this section, we have examined the intricate process of fusing Dynamics 365 Business Central with various systems, adopting a methodical and calculated approach. Utilizing the DREAM structure—Discovery, Requirements, Evaluation, Alignment, and Mapping—we've employed a thorough strategy for managing this integration efficiently.

We highlighted the pivotal role of functional consultants in the Discovery stage, who are responsible for collecting business needs from stakeholders and mapping out the existing business environment. In the Requirements stage, these professionals converted the collected insights into practical integration criteria that resonate with organizational ambitions.

The Evaluation stage played a key role in determining Business Central's technical strengths and limitations, and the Alignment stage was crucial in matching these specifications to both the technical landscape and business aims. The Mapping stage then involved specifying data fields and processes, laying down a definitive guide for the technical team to follow during integration.

We explored leading platforms for integration like Power Automate, Power BI, Microsoft Teams, Outlook, OneNote, LinkedIn's Sales Navigator, Microsoft 365, and Microsoft Exchange. The integration of these platforms leverages the collaborative, analytical, and functional potential of Business Central, optimizing business operations and boosting productivity.

We also addressed the critical role of data synchronization and automation, which are essential for preserving data consistency across platforms and reducing manual efforts. With automated systems and real-time data updates, businesses can enhance precision, operational efficiency, and customer contentment.

In wrapping up this chapter, it's evident that integrating Business Central with other tools transcends mere system connectivity; it revolutionizes business functionality. It's a strategic initiative with the potential to substantially benefit an organization, offering streamlined processes, informed decision-making, enhanced customer interaction, and greater flexibility.

By adhering to the outlined principles and instances, enterprises can anticipate a seamless and adaptable integration process, one that fulfills the vision of a fully integrated business management system. Armed with the foundational insights from this chapter, companies are prepared to undertake their integration ventures with assurance and precision.

KEY HIGHLIGHTS

- Functional consultants map business needs to system requirements.

- Technical consultants ensure the technical viability of integrations.

- The DREAM framework structures the integration process.

- Integrating with platforms like Power BI and Microsoft 365 expands Business Central's capabilities.

- Synchronization and automation are key for data consistency and process efficiency.

- Cross-discipline collaboration is essential for a seamless integration process.

- Stakeholder engagement is crucial for relevant and effective integration outcomes.

- Adherence to security and compliance standards is a must in any integration.

- Practical examples illustrate the tangible benefits of system integration.

- Integration transforms Business Central into a full-fledged business management suite.

CHAPTER 9

Testing and Quality Assurance

This segment delves into the critical significance of systematic testing during the implementation of Business Central, emphasizing the urgency of identifying and rectifying potential system vulnerabilities at an early stage.

Tailored testing procedures are critical for Business Central implementations, as they cater to the specific requirements of individual organizations. An assortment of testing methodologies is utilized, with each one selected to uncover and refine distinct aspects of the system's operation and performance. The ultimate goal is to configure and customize business central that is not only technically flawless but also intricately woven with and conducive to the organization's strategic aspirations.

Quality assurance is not merely a precautionary measure to identify mistakes; rather, it is a comprehensive and proactive process that permeates every phase of system deployment. It entails establishing a framework of best practices and standards to guarantee that each stage, commencing from conception and concluding with implementation, conforms to an exemplary benchmark of reliability, consistency, and distinction.

© Dr. Gomathi S 2024
Dr. Gomathi S, *Mastering Microsoft Dynamics 365 Business Central*,
https://doi.org/10.1007/979-8-8688-0230-0_9

As the discourse progresses, we shall elucidate the intricacies of Quality Assurance and Testing in the context of Business Central. This narrative provides pragmatic perspectives and practical guidance for effectively traversing the critical phases of implementation, encompassing the development of a comprehensive testing strategy and comprehending the range of testing activities necessary for a resilient system. In addition, we shall analyze the intricacies of User Acceptance Testing (UAT), an essential stage which verifies the preparedness of the system for its ultimate users.

Overview

Acquiring proficiency in the evaluation and quality control procedures that are critical for a Business Central implementation is the objective of this chapter. It begins by emphasizing the critical importance of testing in this ecosystem before delving into the variety of testing methodologies that are appropriate for such environments. The subsequent section guides you through the process of developing a strategic test plan, emphasizing the importance of thorough preparation in order to guarantee a seamless and prosperous system introduction.

Significant emphasis is placed on the User Acceptance Testing (UAT) procedure, during which the intricacies of ensuring that the system fulfills the unique requirements of the organization are exposed. This encompasses tactics to actively involve end users throughout the testing stage, request their feedback, and subsequently enhance the system to align with the requirements of the organization.

The primary emphasis of this chapter is on the practical applications of these principles in real-life situations. By doing so, you will be equipped with sound advice and solutions that will strengthen the robustness and precision of your Business Central deployment. The objective of this chapter is to furnish you with the requisite information and resources to effectively carry out the testing and quality assurance phase, thereby establishing a foundation for a Business Central deployment that surpasses all anticipations.

Types of Testing in Business Central Implementation

Testing within the Business Central implementation is an extensive process designed to confirm that the system adheres to functional requirements and operates consistently and effectively across different scenarios.[1]

The primary categories of testing commonly integrated into a Business Central implementation project are as follows[2]:

1. **Unit Testing:**

    - **Description**: Unit testing constitutes the examination of individual components or modules within the Business Central framework. The focus is on the operational integrity of discrete code segments, typically carried out by the developers themselves.

    - **Purpose**: The goal is to ensure that each component of the software works as intended. This is the first phase of testing and aids in the early detection of problems.

    - **Methodology**: For every component or module, developers create test cases. This process can also be aided by automated tools.

---

[1] www.geeksforgeeks.org/types-software-testing/
[2] www.perfecto.io/resources/types-of-testing

2. **Integration Testing:**

- **Description**: This form of testing focuses on the interfaces and interactions between distinct Business Central modules or components.

- **Purpose**: To ensure that the various components of the application work in unison. It is critical for recognizing problems with the interaction of integrated components.

- **Methodology**: Integration testing is often performed following unit testing. Depending on the project requirements, it can be done top-down, bottom-up, or sandwich style.

3. **System Testing:**

- **Description**: Entails validating the entire and fully integrated software product.

- **Purpose**: To ensure that the entire application fits the standards. It is a key stage in ensuring that the system as a whole works properly.

- **Methodology**: This is usually a black-box testing method, where the focus is on the input and output of the system without concerning the internal workings.

4. **Performance Testing:**

- **Description**: Performance testing assesses the speed, responsiveness, and stability of the Business Central system under a particular workload.

- **Purpose**: To ensure the system performs well under expected and peak load conditions. It helps in identifying performance bottlenecks.

- **Methodology**: This includes load testing, stress testing, and sometimes spike testing, to evaluate how the system behaves under different types of strain.

5. **User Acceptance Testing (UAT):**

- **Description**: UAT is a critical phase where the end users test the system to verify if it can handle required tasks in real-world scenarios, according to specifications.

- **Purpose**: To ensure the software can support day-to-day business processes and tasks. It is the final step in testing before the system goes live.

- **Methodology**: Customers are prompted to test the system using real-world circumstances. Their input is critical for making last tweaks before deployment.

6. **Regression Testing:**

- **Description**: This sort of testing guarantees that new code changes have not adversely affected the Business Central system's existing functionality.

- **Purpose**: Confirm that recent program or code changes have not had an adverse effect on current functionalities.

- **Methodology**: This entails re-running functional and non-functional tests to confirm that previously produced and tested software continues to function after a modification.

7. **Systems Integration Test (SIT):**

   Description: Systems Integration Testing involves assessing the integrations between Business Central and other systems. This testing phase focuses on ensuring seamless data exchange and functionality between Business Central and external or complementary systems.

   Purpose: The primary goal is to verify that Business Central integrates effectively with other systems, ensuring data consistency, accurate workflow execution, and overall system interoperability.

   Methodology: Initially, the first level of testing is conducted jointly by the vendors of the integrated systems, followed by testing from the client's side. This approach ensures that both technical and functional aspects of the integration are thoroughly evaluated.

8. **Conference Room Pilot (CRP):**

   Description: The Conference Room Pilot is a comprehensive test of Business Central's functionality against the client's specific requirements. It involves simulating the client's real-world business processes using the actual master files, reference data, and sample transactions.

Purpose: The aim is to validate that Business Central's functionality aligns with the client's needs and business processes. This test is crucial for identifying any discrepancies or areas that require modification.

Methodology: Conducted by the vendor, CRP allows for a detailed review of the system's performance in a controlled environment. Any necessary corrections or adjustments to the solution are identified and made prior to proceeding to the User Acceptance Testing (UAT) phase.

All of these testing methods is critical to ensuring a thorough and successful Business Central installation. They work together to discover and resolve problems, ensuring that the system is resilient, effective, and prepared for deployment in an actual business context.

Table 9-1 provides an organized overview of the many types of testing, emphasizing the balance of functional and technical components while also identifying the important individuals involved in each stage. The examples demonstrate what each sort of testing implies in the setting of Business Central deployment.

Table 9-1. *Overview of Testing Types in Business Central Implementation: Functional and Technical Roles, Stakeholder Involvement, and Examples*

Testing Type	Functional Involvement	Technical Involvement	Other People Involved	Examples
Unit Testing	Minimal	High (Developers)	-	Testing individual functions in the code, like a specific calculation or data retrieval function
Integration Testing	Moderate	High (Developers, QA Engineers)	System Analysts	Testing the data flow between modules, like the integration of the sales module with inventory management
System Testing	High (Business Analysts)	High (QA Engineers)	-	Testing the complete system for requirements compliance, like end-to-end business process flows
Performance Testing	Low	High (Performance Testers)	Infrastructure Specialists	Load testing to check system behavior under peak usage, stress testing for system limits

(*continued*)

Table 9-1. (*continued*)

Testing Type	Functional Involvement	Technical Involvement	Other People Involved	Examples
User Acceptance Testing (UAT)	High (End Users)	Moderate (Supporting Technical Staff)	Business Stakeholders	End users performing real-world tasks to validate the system, like processing an order from start to finish
Regression Testing	Moderate	High (QA Engineers)	-	Re-testing existing functionalities after code changes, like verifying the order process after an update
Security Testing	Low	High (Security Specialists)	Compliance Officers	Penetration testing to identify vulnerabilities, compliance testing for data protection standards
Compatibility Testing	Moderate	High (QA Engineers)	-	Testing the system on different browsers, operating systems, and hardware configurations

(*continued*)

Table 9-1. (*continued*)

Testing Type	Functional Involvement	Technical Involvement	Other People Involved	Examples
Systems Integration Test (SIT)	Moderate	High (Technical Integration Team)	Vendors of Integrated Systems	Testing the integration of Business Central with other systems, like verifying data synchronization with a CRM system
Conference Room Pilot (CRP)	High (Business Process Owners)	Moderate (Implementation Team)	-	Simulating real-world business processes using the client's data, like running through a complete sales cycle to validate functionality

Creating Test Plan

A test plan is an important element in the business central process of implementation. It describes the strategy, resources, duration, and actions needed to guarantee that the new system fulfills your business needs.[3] Here's a step-by-step guide to developing a successful test plan (Figure 9-1):

---

[3] www.guru99.com/what-everybody-ought-to-know-about-test-planing.html

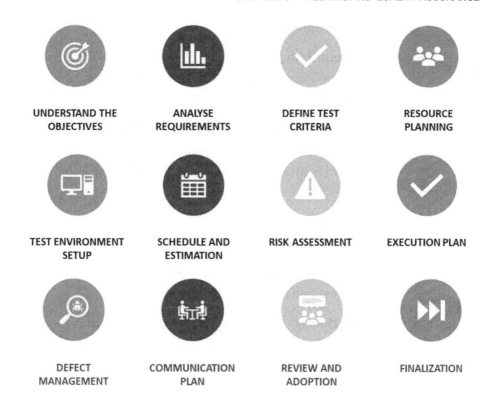

UNDERSTAND THE OBJECTIVES	ANALYSE REQUIREMENTS	DEFINE TEST CRITERIA	RESOURCE PLANNING
TEST ENVIRONMENT SETUP	SCHEDULE AND ESTIMATION	RISK ASSESSMENT	EXECUTION PLAN
DEFECT MANAGEMENT	COMMUNICATION PLAN	REVIEW AND ADOPTION	FINALIZATION

Figure 9-1. *Creating test plan*

1. **Understand the Objectives:**

   • **Define the Scope:** Outline what will be tested, including Business Central components and functionalities.

   • **Establish Objectives:** Determine what testing should accomplish, such as assuring functionality, efficiency, and adherence to business requirements.

2. **Analyze Requirements:**

- **Collect Requirements:** Gather full requirements from stakeholders, encompassing functional, technical, and company demands.

- **Examine Paperwork:** Make certain that all essential paperwork, such as specifications for designs and instructions for use, are accessible and up to date.

3. **Define Test Criteria:**

- **Success Criteria:** Describe what makes for a successful test, such as benchmarks for performance and functionality requirements.

- **Exit Criteria:** Specify the criteria for which testing can be completed, such as a particular stage of defect resolution or compliance with all important requirements.

4. **Resource Planning:**

- **Team Composition:** Identify the roles and responsibilities of the test team members.

- **Tools and Equipment:** Determine the tools (like test management software) and resources (e.g., test environments) desired for testing.

5. **Test Environment Setup:**

- **Configuration:** Set up the gear, Sandbox environments, network, and data in the test environment.

- **Data Preparation:** Ensure that sufficient and relevant test data is accessible or prepared for an efficient testing process.

6. **Design Test Cases:**

    - Create extensive test cases covering all areas of the system's functionality.

    - **Assess and Approve:** Have stakeholders assess the test cases for completeness and relevancy.

7. **Schedule and Estimation:**

    - **Timeline:** Create a precise timetable for testing activities, complete with milestones and deadlines.

    - **Estimate Effort:** To efficiently allocate resources, determine the amount of time needed for each testing activity.

8. **Risk Assessment:**

    - **Identifying Threats:** Analyze possible threats in the procedure for testing, such as a lack of resources or technical challenges.

    - **Risk Mitigation Ways:** Create ways to reduce identified risks.

9. **Execution Plan:**

    - **Test Execution:** Describe how to execute test cases, covering the order of execution and dependencies.

    - **Monitoring and Control:** Create methods for tracking test progress and directing testing activities.

10. **Defect Management:**

- **Tracking:** Implement a system for tracking and managing defects identified during testing.

- **Resolution Process:** Define the process for addressing and resolving defects.

11. **Communication Plan:**

- **Reporting:** Determine the reporting structure and frequency for test progress and results.

- **Stakeholder Engagement:** Ensure continuous engagement with stakeholders throughout the testing process.

12. **Review and Adaptation:**

- **Incessant Enhancement:** Review the test process on a regular basis and adapt as needed to address issues and changes in requirements.

13. **Finalization:**

- **Closure Report:** Create the last closure report that summarizes the testing operations, results, and any outstanding issues.

- **Lessons learnt:** For future reference, document lessons learnt and best practices.

A thorough test plan is required for the effective execution of Business Central. It ensures that all components of the system have been properly tested and that any faults have been detected and addressed before the system is put into operation. This procedure necessitates meticulous preparation, organization, and communication among all parties.

Creating Test Plan

Preparing a test plan in table style might aid in organizing and presenting information more effectively. In a tabular style, here's an example of how you would organize a test plan for a Business Central implementation.

Table 9-2. *The Test plan template*

Section	Details
Test Plan ID	BC_TP_01
Introduction	A summary of the Business Central deployment and the goals of this test plan
Test Items	Items to be tested include individual modules such as sales, purchasing, and finance
Features to be Tested	Detailed list of features and functionalities that will be covered in the testing
Features Not to be Tested	Any areas or features that are out of scope for this test plan
Approach	Overview of the testing strategy, including types of testing to be performed (e.g., unit testing, integration testing, UAT)
Pass/Fail Criteria	Definition of what constitutes a pass or fail outcome for each test
Suspension Criteria and Resumption Requirements	Conditions under which testing will be suspended and the requirements for resumption
Test Deliverables	List of documents and reports to be delivered as part of the testing process (e.g., test cases, defect reports)
Testing Tasks	Detailed tasks that need to be completed as part of the testing process

(continued)

Table 9-2. (*continued*)

Section	Details
Environmental Needs	Sandbox environments and network settings are required for the test environment
Responsibilities	Each team member's role and responsibilities in the testing process
Staffing and Training Needs	Any staffing or training requirements for the testing team
Schedule	Testing activity timeline, covering the beginning and ending date for every stage of testing
Risks and Contingencies	Identification of potential hazards and preparation for contingencies
Approval	The test plan requires signatures. Final Stage

Security Evaluations in Business Central

Permission Evaluation

Insight: In the context of Dynamics 365 Business Central, Permission Evaluation is a crucial process that occurs during the User Acceptance Testing (UAT) stage. It involves a thorough assessment of user roles and permissions within the system.

Intention: The primary objective of this evaluation is to ensure that each user or role within the system is granted only the necessary permissions. This is vital for maintaining operational integrity and preventing unauthorized access or misuse of the system.

Technique: The process involves reviewing and verifying user roles and the permissions assigned to them. This includes checking access levels to different modules and functionalities within Business Central, ensuring that they align with the user's job requirements and responsibilities.

Backup, Disaster Recovery, High Availability, and Geo-replication Evaluation

Insight: Dynamics 365 Business Central offers standard features for Backup, Disaster Recovery (DR), High Availability, and Geo-replication. Evaluating these features is essential to ensure business continuity and data integrity.

Intention: The aim is to assess the system's capability to handle data backup, recover from disasters, maintain high availability, and manage data replication across geographical locations. This ensures that the system remains operational and data is secure, even in the event of unexpected disruptions.

Technique: The evaluation involves reviewing the backup and disaster recovery plans provided by Microsoft, understanding the high availability setup, and examining the geo-replication capabilities. This includes testing the backup restoration process, simulating disaster recovery scenarios, and ensuring that there is no data loss or system downtime during these processes.

Compatibility Verification

Insight: In the context of Dynamics 365 Business Central, a SaaS product, compatibility verification is centered around ensuring that client systems meet the certified minimum requirements as documented by Microsoft. This includes compatibility with specific web browsers, mobile operating systems, and other system requirements essential for optimal functionality.

Intention: The primary purpose is to confirm that client systems are updated and aligned with Microsoft's recommended configurations. This ensures that Business Central maintains its optimal functionality and security in the operational environment.

Technique: The verification process involves checking that the client's web browsers and mobile operating systems are upgraded to the versions certified by Microsoft. This is crucial for ensuring not only compatibility but also the security and performance of Business Central. While Business Central may operate on browsers or versions not officially documented, it is strongly advised against using such configurations due to potential security vulnerabilities and performance issues.

Critical Consideration: All these testing methods are integral to a thorough and successful Business Central installation. They collectively ensure that the system is resilient, effective, and ready for deployment in a real business environment. Adhering to Microsoft's documented system requirements is a key step in this process, providing a foundation for a secure and efficient operation of Business Central.

Summary

It is essential, to consider the critical importance of quality assurance and testing to the effective implementation of Business Central. During this expedition, we have examined the diverse categories of testing that are imperative for guaranteeing a resilient and dependable system. These include user acceptability and security testing, unit and integration testing, and more. Every category of testing fulfills a distinct function, and when combined, they constitute a holistic strategy for detecting and rectifying potential problems.

The development of an elaborate test strategy proved to be a critical milestone in this endeavor. By acting as a strategic guide, it directs the testing team through each stage of the testing process, guaranteeing that each element of the system is thoroughly examined and verified in relation to the business prerequisites. Emphasis on explicit communication, risk management, resource allocation, and scheduling within the plan emphasizes the need for a methodical and structured approach to testing.

In addition, we explored the pragmatic elements of test case design, emphasizing the significance of test scenarios that are unambiguous, succinct, and all-encompassing, encompassing a vast array of system functionalities. The test cases serve as the foundation of a successful testing strategy, guaranteeing a comprehensive evaluation of every element of the Business Central system.

During this phase, the participation of numerous stakeholders is critical, including technical teams, functional experts, and end users. Their collective effort guarantees that the system is not solely technically flawless, but also in accordance with the practical requirements of the organization. User Acceptance Testing (UAT) is a critical stage during which the system is examined in practical situations to verify that it fulfills the requirements and anticipations of the end users.

In conclusion, this chapter emphasizes the significance of a thorough and effectively implemented testing and quality assurance strategy during the implementation of Business Central. An essential investment that yields favorable outcomes in the shape of a dependable, effective, and intuitive system. Through a comprehensive evaluation process that guarantees adherence to the most stringent quality criteria, organizations can with assurance utilize Business Central to accomplish their operational objectives and foster triumph.

As we progress, keep in mind that the purpose of testing and quality assurance is not solely to identify and resolve issues; rather, it is to instill trust in the system and guarantee a seamless, fruitful transition to a novel approach to overseeing business processes. You are now endowed with the knowledge and approaches delineated in this chapter to effectively maneuver through the testing stage of your Business Central implementation. This will ensure a prosperous deployment and establish a strong groundwork for your organization's activities.

KEY HIGHLIGHTS

1. **Significance of Testing and Quality Control:** Understood the crucial importance of quality assurance and testing in guaranteeing the triumphant implementation of Business Central.

2. **Types of Testing:**

   - **Unit Testing:** Testing individual components or modules.

   - **Integration Testing:** Ensuring different modules work together seamlessly.

   - **System Testing:** Validating the complete and fully integrated software product.

   - **Performance Testing:** Assessing the system's performance under various conditions.

   - **User Acceptance Testing (UAT):** Confirming the system meets user requirements and business processes.

   - **Regression Testing:** Regression testing is a critical process that verifies the absence of negative impacts on extant functionalities caused by new changes.

   - **Security Testing:** Identifying vulnerabilities to secure the system.

   - **Compatibility Testing:** Checking the system's compatibility with different environments.

3. **Formulating an Exhaustive Test Plan:** Exhaustive direction on formulating an all-encompassing test plan that addresses risks, aims, scope, resources, plan, and test environment configuration.

4. **Test Case Design:** Guidelines for constructing efficient test cases, encompassing the establishment of preconditions, test steps, anticipated outcomes, and documentation of results.

5. **Stakeholder Involvement:** Emphasizing the participation of diverse stakeholders in the testing procedure, such as technical teams, functional specialists, and end users.

6. **User Acceptance Testing (UAT):** An in-depth analysis of UAT, with a particular focus on its significance within the broader testing methodology.

7. **Strategies for Controlling and Tracking Test Activities:** Methods for efficiently overseeing the advancement of testing activities and regulating their diverse facets.

8. **Defect Management:** A discourse on the procedures entailed in the monitoring, control, and resolution of defects that are discovered throughout the testing phase.

9. **Communication and Reporting:** During the testing process, the significance of effective communication and consistent reporting cannot be overstated.

10. **Evaluation and Adjustment:** The imperative nature of consistently evaluating and modifying the test plan and test cases in order to confront obstacles and modifications in project specifications.

Conclude the Test Plan: Instructions on concluding the test plan, which entails the compilation of a closure report and the documentation of insights gained.

EXERCISE

Exercise Exercise 1: Test Case Development

Practical application of the knowledge gained regarding test case development is the objective.

Objective: Select a particular Business Central module or functionality, such as the Sales Order process. Construct an exhaustive test scenario for this functionality. The components of a test case consist of the following: test case ID, title, outline, prerequisites, test steps, expected results, and annotations pertaining to any particular data requirements.

Outcome: An exhaustive test case document for a selected Business Central functionality.

Exercise 2: Develop an Outline of a Test Plan

Understanding the structure and constituents of a test plan is the objective.

Objective: Develop a test plan outline for the implementation of Business Central. Introduction, Test Items, Features to be Tested, Test Environment, Roles and Responsibilities, Schedule, and Risk Management are some of the sections that should be included.

Outcome: A delineated framework of a test plan that showcases comprehension of the fundamental elements and their significance.

Exercise 3: User Acceptance Testing (UAT) through Role-Playing

Gaining an understanding of the significance of the UAT process is the objective.

Objective: Assign responsibilities such as Business Central users, project managers, and IT support personnel in a group setting. Conduct a role-playing exercise of a UAT scenario in which "users" evaluate and provide feedback on a particular Business Central process.

Result: A simulated user acceptance testing (UAT) session, with an emphasis on the implementation team and end users' interactions.

CHAPTER 10

Go-Live and Post-implementation Support

Initiating the Go-Live phase in the deployment of Business Central signifies a pivotal shift from the theoretical framework of projects to the tangible realities of everyday use. This stage represents the zenith of extensive strategizing, crafting, and verification, all converging into a defining moment when the system transitions into active service. The seamless execution of Go-Live reflects the thoroughness and exactitude invested in the preparatory stages. Yet, this milestone isn't a finale; it heralds the commencement of an ongoing journey focused on maintaining and boosting the system's efficacy through proactive post-implementation support and upkeep.[1]

The onset of the Go-Live stage is marked by an atmosphere charged with expectation and detailed examination, as each component of the Business Central system undergoes rigorous testing within the operational business setting. Successfully navigating the challenges during this pivotal time is critical for a fluid shift to the new system, thereby preventing any

---

[1] https://learn.microsoft.com/en-us/training/modules/post-go-live-dynamics-365/

© Dr. Gomathi S 2024
Dr. Gomathi S, *Mastering Microsoft Dynamics 365 Business Central*,
https://doi.org/10.1007/979-8-8688-0230-0_10

interruption to standard business activities. What follows is the phase of post-implementation support, which is dedicated to crafting a sustainable model for continual enhancement and equipping the organization with the tools to address any emerging issues post-launch.

Such a phase demands a thoughtful and strategic approach to guarantee that the system does more than just function; it must evolve in tandem with the changing needs of the business. With steadfast support, the investment in Business Central promises to yield ongoing returns, securing the system's place as a valuable asset for the organization's progression.

Overview

This chapter probes into the essential phases of Go-Live and the subsequent support for Business Central. It equips readers with the insights needed for meticulous Go-Live preparations, emphasizing strategies for a smooth operational transition. The chapter then navigates through the typical hurdles encountered during Go-Live, providing guidance on surmounting these obstacles to preserve operational flow.

Transitioning to post-implementation, the narrative shifts to detail the integral elements of adept support and upkeep strategies. It discusses the optimal practices for delivering consistent user support, managing system enhancements, and ensuring that the Business Central setup remains attuned to the evolving ambitions and expansion of the organization. This chapter is crafted to furnish readers with the acumen required to successfully steer through the Go-Live stage and to continue enhancing system utility and investment value over time.

Preparing for Go-Live

As we approach the Go-Live stage for Business Central, it's crucial to focus on the meticulous assignment of user permissions and access in the production environment. This step is more than just a routine task; it's a safeguard against unauthorized access and a means to ensure that each user has the appropriate level of system entry to fulfill their roles effectively.

Alongside configuring system settings and conducting user training, a significant emphasis must be placed on the careful allocation of user licenses. This involves not only acquiring additional licenses as needed but also strategically assigning them to the team members. It's a process that demands thoughtful consideration, balancing the organization's operational requirements with budgetary constraints.

Equally important is the preliminary step of having all users log in to Business Central before the official Go-Live date. This initial login serves a twofold purpose: verifying the correct setup of user accounts and providing users with an early orientation to the new system, thus mitigating potential login issues during the critical Go-Live period.

These essential activities, together with robust system testing, accurate data migration, and the formulation of comprehensive cutover and communication plans, are the pillars of a solid Go-Live strategy. By giving these areas the attention they deserve, organizations can ensure a smooth and successful transition to Business Central, paving the way for a seamless operational shift.

Key Activities in Preparing for Go-Live:

1. **Final System Testing:** Before the Go-Live event, it's imperative to carry out a range of conclusive tests to verify the proper functioning of all business operations. This should cover comprehensive system-wide testing, user acceptance testing (UAT), and regression testing to ascertain that recent modifications haven't negatively impacted the pre-existing features.

2. **User Training and Documentation:** It's important to facilitate sufficient training for the end users to make sure they are at ease with the new system. The training must be thorough, tailored to the specific roles, and should equip users with the essential materials and documentation for future reference after the training concludes.

3. **Cutover Plan:** The transition blueprint, or cutover plan, outlines the meticulous steps for the launch. It encompasses schedules, designated roles, duties, and backup strategies. This plan needs to be disseminated among all involved parties and must detail the method of shifting from the legacy system to the new one.

4. **Down Time/System Freeze Plan:** Before initiating the data migration, it is crucial to implement a System Freeze or Down Time plan for the current system. This plan is designed to halt all operations and data entry in the existing system, ensuring that no new data is introduced during the migration process. The System Freeze is a critical step as it guarantees that the data snapshot transferred to Business Central is accurate and complete, reflecting the most current state of the business operations up to that point. The plan should detail the duration of the freeze, the specific steps to enforce it, and the procedures to ensure that all system users are aware of and adhere to the freeze. It's a safeguard to maintain data integrity and prevent discrepancies during the transition.

5. **Data Migration and Validation:** The process of data migration is a sensitive one, involving the transfer of all critical data from old systems to Business Central. Ensuring this data's correctness and completeness is essential to avoid complications when the system goes live.

6. **Communication Plan:** A well-defined and straightforward communication strategy guarantees that everyone involved is aware of the Go-Live timeline, what is anticipated of them, and any necessary steps they need to take. It also covers the protocols for communication during the Go-Live phase, including guidance on seeking assistance or reporting problems.[2]

7. **Contingency and Risk Mitigation:** Recognizing possible hazards and devising fallback strategies is essential. This may include preparing a rollback strategy to revert to the previous system if significant problems emerge during the Go-Live that cannot be promptly remedied.

8. **System Freeze and Backup:** It is common practice to set up a system freeze prior to coming live, during which no additional changes are made. Furthermore, it is crucial to ensure which all data is backed up prior to the transition, in case a rollback becomes necessary.

---

[2] https://learn.microsoft.com/en-us/dynamics365/guidance/implementation-guide/prepare-to-go-live

9. **Go-Live Support Structure:** It is critical to establish a system of assistance for the Go-Live phase. During the transition, this includes IT support, a dedicated helpdesk, and the availability of super users in critical areas to resolve any technical problems that may arise.

During the preparation phase, perseverance and focus to detail are crucial. Ensure that all stakeholders are prepared, attend to any remaining concerns, and lay the groundwork for a prosperous transformation to the new Business Central system. The level of effort dedicated to Go-Live preparation can have a substantial impact on the smoothness and achievement of the Go-Live itself.

Key Roles and Responsibilities in Preparing for Business Central Go-Live

Various organizational roles are typically tasked with the responsibility of preparing for the Go-Live phase, with each role playing a vital role in guaranteeing a seamless transition to the newly implemented Business Central system. The responsibilities of the following essential stakeholders are outlined:

Project Manager (PM): Supervises and ensures timely completion of all activities throughout the Go-Live phase. The PM oversees resource availability and allocation, administers the project plan, and coordinates between various teams.

Business Analysts (BAs): Their comprehension of business requirements and verification that the system has been configured to fulfill these needs are of utmost importance. Additionally, BAs participate in the development of test cases and may aid in user training.

IT/System Administrators: Entrusted with the technical configuration, encompassing backups, security protocols, server readiness, and system configurations. During Go-Live, they may also provide assistance in resolving technical issues and managing data migration.

Data Migration Specialists: Assist in the transfer of data from legacy systems to Business Central, with a particular emphasis on post-migration validation and assurance of data integrity.

Responsibility of Training Coordinators: Coordinate and lead training sessions for end users. They guarantee that every user is provided with the essential training and resources required to proficiently operate the newly implemented system.

End Users: While not accountable for the preparatory phase, end users assume a crucial function during the Go-Live operation. It is critical to incorporate their suggestions through user acceptance testing in order to resolve any operational issues.

Quality Assurance (QA) Team: Responsible for ensuring the system functions as intended through the execution of numerous tests. They verify the system's functionality, performance, and security.

Change Management Team: Obligatory for informing all stakeholders regarding forthcoming modifications, furnishing assistance and resources to facilitate change management, and guaranteeing that the organization is adequately prepared to adopt the new system.

Help Desk Personnel: Establishes the necessary support infrastructure to aid users throughout and following the Go-Live phase. They guarantee the availability of assistance resources to address any challenges that users might confront.

In addition to the outlined roles, the involvement of "Champions" is integral to the Go-Live process. Champions are selected individuals from within the team who act as First Responders to their department or group. They play a crucial role in boosting confidence in the new system among their peers. By attending specialized workshops, Champions are equipped to handle queries and concerns from their team members efficiently and are prepared to escalate any significant system issues that may arise. Their presence is pivotal in fostering a smooth transition, as they serve as the immediate point of contact for their teams, bridging the gap between end users and the technical support team.

Functional Consultants also play a critical role during the Go-Live phase. They step in to address and resolve issues that emerge, particularly those related to the system's functionality. Their deep understanding of Business Central's features and business processes makes them adept at troubleshooting problems and implementing solutions that align with the organization's operational needs.

Technical Consultants, on the other hand, are essential for resolving issues related to system customizations and integrations. Their technical expertise is crucial for identifying and fixing any bugs or glitches that may occur in the custom-developed features or when integrating Business Central with other systems. Their role ensures that the technical aspects of the system are functioning smoothly and as intended, minimizing disruptions to business operations.

The success of the Go-Live event hinges on the collaborative efforts of all these roles. Champions, Functional Consultants, and Technical Consultants each bring a unique set of skills and expertise that complement the efforts of Project Managers, Business Analysts, IT/System Administrators, and other key stakeholders. Together, they form a comprehensive support network that ensures the system, processes, and people are well-aligned and prepared for a successful transition to the new Business Central system. Effective communication and well-defined responsibilities among these roles are vital for navigating the complexities of Go-Live and ensuring its success.

Refer to Table 10-1 to get an overview of Roles of Functional and Technical Consultants in Business Central Go-Live Preparation.

Table 10-1. *Roles of Functional and Technical Consultants in Business Central Go-Live Preparation*

Functional Consultant Responsibilities	Technical Consultant Responsibilities
Requirement Validation	**System Configuration**
Confirming that all business requirements are accurately translated into the system setup	Setting up and configuring the technical environment for Business Central
Process Mapping	**Data Migration**
Ensuring business processes are correctly reflected within the system	Executing the transfer of data from old systems to Business Central and ensuring its integrity
User Training and Documentation	**Custom Development**
Developing training materials and conducting training sessions for end users	Developing custom solutions, extensions, or integrations required by the business
User Acceptance Testing (UAT)	Performance Tuning
Leading the UAT to ensure the system meets business needs	Optimizing system performance and ensuring stability
Change Management	**Technical Troubleshooting**
Assisting in managing the transition to the new system and user adoption	Diagnosing and solving technical problems that arise during Go-Live
Support and Help Desk Training	**Security and Compliance**

(*continued*)

Table 10-1. (*continued*)

Functional Consultant Responsibilities	Technical Consultant Responsibilities
Training the support team on business	Ensuring that the system meets
processes to assist users post-Go-Live	security standards and compliance
	requirements
Feedback Coordination	**Backup and Recovery Planning**
Gathering and incorporating user	Setting up backup procedures and
feedback during UAT to improve system	disaster recovery plans
functionality	
Go-Live Readiness Assessment	**Infrastructure Readiness**
Assessing whether the business is ready	Ensuring all hardware and software
to transition to the new system	infrastructure is in place and operational for Go-Live

Addressing Challenges During Go-Live

The Go-Live phase of a Business Central implementation is a pivotal moment when the system is transitioned into active use. Despite thorough preparation, organizations may encounter unexpected challenges that can disrupt this critical phase. Addressing these challenges swiftly and effectively is key to a successful Go-Live.

Common Challenges and Strategies for Addressing Them:

1. **User Resistance and Adaptation:** Even with thorough training, users may resist the new system due to comfort with the old processes or fear of the unknown.

   - **Strategy:** Reinforce change management efforts, provide additional support and resources, and establish a feedback loop where users can voice concerns and receive assistance.

2. **Data Integrity Issues:** Migrated data might present inconsistencies or errors when it goes live, leading to operational hiccups.

   - **Strategy:** Implement rigorous pre-Go-Live data checks and have a data specialist team on standby to address any issues promptly.

3. **Technical Glitches:** Unexpected software bugs or hardware issues can arise, causing system slowdowns or outages.

   - **Strategy:** Have IT support and technical consultants readily available to troubleshoot and resolve issues as they occur.

4. **Performance Problems:** The system may experience performance issues when faced with the full load of live operational data and concurrent users.

   - **Strategy:** Conduct load testing before Go-Live and monitor system performance continuously, ready to optimize and scale resources as needed.

5. **Process Misalignment:** Business processes may not align perfectly with the new system, leading to confusion or delays.

   - **Strategy:** Work with functional consultants to review processes and provide immediate guidance or adjustments to fit the new system.

6. **Insufficient Training:** Users might find themselves inadequately prepared to use the new system effectively, leading to errors and reduced productivity.

   - **Strategy:** Offer just-in-time training sessions and quick reference materials to enhance user competence and confidence.

7. **Communication Defect:** Inadequate communication regarding the newly implemented system and processes may result in inaccurate or insufficient information.

   - **Strategy:** Ensure consistent and transparent communication channels are maintained throughout the entire organization, and furnish periodic updates.

8. **Insufficient Support Systems:** The lack of a comprehensive support network can engender a sense of isolation among users, exacerbating the strain associated with the transition.

   - **Approach:** Form an all-encompassing Go-Live support team comprising help desk personnel, IT support, and super users.

Through proactive anticipation of potential obstacles and the implementation of contingency strategies, organizations can more effectively navigate the intricacies associated with Go-Live. The objective is to reduce interruptions, guarantee uninterrupted operations, and establish a nurturing atmosphere that promotes rapid acclimation to the novel Business Central system.

Best Practices for a Smooth Go-Live Transition in Business Central Implementation

Structured Go-Live Plan for Business Central Implementation

A Structured Go-Live Plan (SGP) is an all-encompassing strategy that is specifically crafted to provide direction to the organization during the pivotal period when the Business Central system is being activated. The document is an intricately designed blueprint that delineates each stage of the Go-Live phase, guaranteeing that all involved parties are cognizant of their respective obligations and are able to follow the process with minimal interruption.

Components of a Structured Go-Live Plan

1. **Project Timeline**: The Go-Live date ought to be explicitly delineated in the plan, accompanied by an elaborate timetable the day before and after this milestone. It should specify significant milestones, including the conclusion of user training, the final data migration, and the date of system freeze.

2. **Delineation of Roles and Responsibilities**: It is imperative to establish unambiguous roles and responsibilities for the business users, external partners, and internal project team. It should be clear to every stakeholder what is anticipated of them and by what date.

3. **Communication Protocols**: In order to guarantee that all parties are apprised of the progress and any modifications to the plan, it is imperative to establish a communication strategy. It is essential to specify the method of update dissemination, the recipients, and the frequency of updates.

4. **System and Data Readiness**: This phase encompasses concluding verifications of the system's configuration and the validation of all data migration operations. It comprises an all-item inventory that must be completed prior to Go-Live.

5. **Instruction and Assistance**: It is imperative that the strategy verifies that every user has received sufficient training and that support systems, including a help desk and super users, are operational and prepared to provide aid throughout and following the Go-Live phase.

6. **Technical and Functional Checks**: Technological consultants ought to conduct concluding assessments of the system's infrastructure, security, and efficiency prior to the go-live phase. Concurrently, functional consultants ought to validate the operations of business processes within Business Central.

7. **Cutover Activities**: The comprehensive cutover strategy outlines the strict order of occurrences that will transpire throughout the Go-Live phase. It should detail the precise procedures that must be followed in order to migrate data from the legacy system to Business Central, as well as the sequences by which the system can be restarted.

8. **Contingency Plans**: The absence of a fallback renders no plan holistic. Contingency plans specify actions to be taken in the case of an accident or setback. This may entail reverting to the previous system or transitioning to a staggered Go-Live strategy.

9. **Risk Management**: Identifying potential risks and creating mitigation strategies is an essential part of the Go-Live plan. It should outline how to handle various scenarios that could derail the Go-Live process.

10. **Post-Go-Live Activities**: The plan should extend beyond the Go-Live date, outlining the activities for the stabilization period, such as monitoring system performance, addressing user issues, and gathering feedback for continuous improvement.

Execution of the Go-Live Plan

- **Rehearsals**: Conduct dry runs or dress rehearsals of the Go-Live to ensure that all parties know exactly what to do when the time comes.

- **Monitoring**: Set up monitoring tools and dashboards that can provide real-time insights into system performance and user activity during Go-Live.

- **Feedback Loops:** Implement mechanisms to gather immediate feedback from users to address any issues they encounter quickly.

The Structured Go-Live Plan for a Business Central implementation is a living document that may be adjusted as needed, but its core purpose remains to guide the organization through a critical period of change with confidence and control.

Note   Structure go-live plan in the Appendix E and F.

Phased Rollout

A phased rollout means implementing the new system in stages, rather than all at once. This approach can minimize risk and disruption because it allows for

- Focused attention on individual modules or departments at a time

- Easier identification and resolution of issues before they become widespread

- Gradual adjustment for users and IT staff, reducing resistance and stress

- The ability to learn from each phase, improving subsequent rollouts

In Business Central, a phased approach might involve rolling out core financial modules first, followed by inventory management, and then sales and service management modules in sequence.

Dry Runs

Dry runs, or dress rehearsals, are trial runs of the Go-Live process. They aim to

- Simulate the Go-Live environment as closely as possible.

- Identify issues with workflows, data migration, and system performance.

- Train the project team on the Go-Live process, making actual deployment smoother.

- Provide an opportunity to test failovers and backups.

In Business Central, a dry run would simulate daily operations, processing transactions using the new system to ensure that all business processes work as expected.

Robust Testing

Comprehensive testing ensures the system is ready for Go-Live. Different types of testing include

- **User Acceptance Testing (UAT):** Validates the solution with actual end users to ensure it meets business requirements.

- **System Integration Testing:** Ensures that Business Central integrates seamlessly with other enterprise applications.

- **Performance Testing:** Checks that the system can handle the required load and performs well under peak conditions.

A robust testing strategy ensures that the system is reliable, scalable, and secure upon Go-Live.

User Training and Documentation

Proper training and clear documentation are the backbones of user readiness:

- Training should be role-based, covering specific tasks that users will perform in Business Central.

- Documentation, FAQs, and quick reference guides should be easily accessible and written in user-friendly language.

- Consider using a mix of training methods, including in-person sessions, webinars, and self-service learning portals.

Support and Communication Channels

Effective support and clear communication are vital during Go-Live:

- A helpdesk should be available to field user queries and issues promptly.

- User forums and instant response teams can provide peer support and rapid problem-solving.

- Regular updates and clear communication from the project team can help manage expectations and reduce anxiety.

Monitoring and Feedback Loop

Active monitoring and a feedback loop provide real-time insight into how the system and users are coping:

- System monitoring tools can track performance, usage, and errors in Business Central.

- User feedback mechanisms can capture user experiences and issues, allowing for quick adjustments and improvements.

Change Management

Managing the human element of change is crucial for success:

- Communicate the benefits of Business Central to all stakeholders to foster buy-in.

- Address resistance by involving users in the transition process and listening to their concerns.

- Recognize and reward cooperation and positive behaviors to reinforce the change.

Post-Go-Live Support

Intense support after Go-Live ensures that users do not feel abandoned:

- Plan for an increased volume of support queries immediately after Go-Live.

- Staff the helpdesk with knowledgeable personnel familiar with Business Central.

- Schedule follow-up training sessions to address common issues and provide additional guidance.

This detailed planning and execution at every step will not only pave the way for a smoother Go-Live but also ensure that Business Central is embraced and effectively utilized by the organization.

Post-implementation Support and Maintenance

Post-implementation support and maintenance are crucial for the long-term success and optimization of a Business Central implementation.[3] After the Go-Live phase, the focus shifts to ensuring the system continues to meet the business's evolving needs and that users receive the support they require to effectively use the new system. Here's a detailed look at the components of post-implementation support and maintenance[4]:

1. **User Support:**

    • **Establish a Helpdesk**: Provide users with a central point of contact for reporting issues and seeking assistance.

    • **Create Support Documentation**: Continuously update FAQs, user guides, and knowledge bases as new questions and issues arise.

    • **Offer Training**: Continuous learning opportunities for users should be provided to enhance their skills as they grow more accustomed to the system.

    Support Contract and Service Management:

    • **Response Times and Service Level Agreements (SLAs)**: Clearly defined response times for various issues as per the SLAs in the support contract.

---

[3] www.compusoftadvisors.com/microsoft-dynamics-post-implementation-support/

[4] www.the365people.com/en-ie/implementation

- **Issue Severity Categorization**: A system for categorizing issue severity to prioritize support tasks effectively.

- **Escalation Management**: Detailed escalation process for unresolved issues as outlined in the support contract.

- **Remote Support Tools**: Identification of tools and platforms used by the vendor for remote support.

- **Support Request Portals**: A dedicated portal for lodging and tracking support requests.

- **Business Hours of the Support Contract**: Defined operational hours for support as per the negotiated contract, ensuring alignment with the organization's operational needs.

2. **System Maintenance:**

- **Perform Regular Updates**: Apply patches and updates from Microsoft to keep Business Central up to date with the latest features and security enhancements.

- **Monitor System Performance**: Use monitoring tools to track system performance and identify areas that may require optimization.

- **Database Maintenance**: Conduct routine inspections to verify the database's integrity and performance, as well as assure that it is backed up and appropriately indexed.

3. **Feature Utilization:**

- **Assess New Functionality**: In the course of Business Central's development, evaluate and integrate new functionalities that have the potential to benefit the organization.

- **User Feedback**: So as to ascertain the way the system has been utilized and identify potential requirements for new features or modifications, gather and evaluate user feedback.

4. **Continuous Improvement:**

- **Process Optimization**: Revisit and refine business processes to ensure they remain aligned with company goals and are fully leveraging Business Central's capabilities.

- **Custom Development**: Develop customizations or integrations as needed to enhance functionality and fit unique business requirements.

5. **Issue Resolution:**

- **Proactive Issue Management**: Identify and resolve issues before they impact business operations, potentially using predictive analytics and AI tools.

- **Change Management**: Manage and document changes to the system to maintain control and history of the evolution of your Business Central environment.

6. **Training and Knowledge Transfer:**

- **Onboard New Users**: As the organization grows and changes, new users will require training.

- **Cross-Training**: Cross-train existing users to ensure that knowledge is not siloed within the organization.

7. **Compliance and Security:**

- **Regular Audits**: Conduct regular audits to ensure that the system complies with regulatory requirements.

- **Security Monitoring**: Continuously monitor security, manage user access controls, and respond to threats.

8. **Vendor Management:**

- **Manage Relationships**: Maintain a good relationship with Microsoft and other vendors for support and information on upcoming changes or issues.

- **License Management**: Regularly review and manage licenses to ensure the organization only pays for what it needs.

9. **Budgeting for IT Expenditure:**

- **Plan for Upgrades**: Set aside budget for future upgrades or unexpected expenditures that may arise from system enhancements or necessary changes.

10. **Reporting and Analytics:**

- **Enhance Reporting**: Utilize Business Central's reporting capabilities to provide insightful analytics and reports to help with decision-making.

11. **Review Meetings:**

- **Schedule Regular Reviews**: Have periodic meetings with key stakeholders to review system performance, user satisfaction, and the value it's bringing to the organization.

Effective post-implementation support and maintenance ensure that the Business Central system remains an asset that drives business growth, rather than a static tool that becomes obsolete. It involves a mix of technical expertise, user support, and strategic planning to maintain the health and utility of the system.

Integrating ITIL and PDSA Methodologies for Effective Post-implementation Support and Maintenance of Business Central

Post-implementation support and maintenance are critical phases where methodologies and techniques ensure the ongoing health and optimization of the implemented system. While there isn't a universally accepted acronym specifically for post-implementation methodology, organizations often adopt a blend of industry-standard methodologies, adapting them to their specific needs.

The choice of methodology for post-implementation support and maintenance of Business Central largely depends on the specific needs, size, and maturity of the organization's IT processes. However, ITIL and PDSA[5] are particularly well-suited for managing the lifecycle of an ERP system like Business Central due to their focus on service management and continuous improvement.

---

[5]www.techtarget.com/whatis/definition/PDCA-plan-do-check-act

ITIL for Business Central Example:

Service Operation:

- **Incident Management:** Implement a system where users can report issues they encounter with Business Central. IT support then categorizes and prioritizes these incidents and works towards resolution.

- **Problem Management:** Identify recurring issues and investigate the underlying problems causing these incidents. Develop long-term solutions to prevent future occurrences.

Continual Service Improvement (CSI):

- Regularly gather feedback from users on the functionality and performance of Business Central.

- Analyze usage patterns and support tickets to identify areas for improvement.

- Implement changes to configurations or customizations within Business Central to enhance user experience and system efficiency.

PDSA for Business Central Example:

Plan:

- Identify that users are struggling with the sales order processing feature in Business Central.

- Plan a targeted training session to improve proficiency and a review of the related documentation.

Do:

- Conduct the training session for a small group of users and update the documentation based on the identified gaps.

Study:

- Measure the effectiveness by evaluating the speed and accuracy of sales order entries post-training.

- Collect feedback from the participants to understand the training's impact.

Act:

- If the intervention is successful, roll out the updated training and documentation to all users.

- If issues persist, analyze the feedback and plan a new approach.

RACI for Business Central Example:

- **Responsible:** Support team members are responsible for responding to user queries related to Business Central.

- **Accountable:** The IT Service Manager is accountable for the overall performance and user satisfaction of Business Central.

- **Consulted:** Business analysts and super users are consulted when significant changes to Business Central processes are proposed.

- **Informed:** All Business Central users are informed about updates, maintenance windows, and new features.

COBIT for Business Central Example:

- **Align, Plan, and Organize:** Ensure that Business Central supports business goals by aligning its functionalities with strategic objectives.

- **Build, Acquire, and Implement:** When a need for a new Business Central module arises, follow a structured process to implement it, ensuring it meets the specific business requirements.

- **Deliver, Service, and Support:** Manage Business Central services by establishing SLAs, monitoring performance, and providing ongoing user support.

KCS^{SM} for Business Central Example:

- **Capture:** When a support issue is resolved, document the solution in a knowledge base article.

- **Structure:** Organize the knowledge base in a user-friendly manner, categorizing articles by Business Central modules and common tasks.

- **Reuse:** Encourage users to consult the knowledge base before raising support tickets.

- **Improve:** Regularly review and update the knowledge base based on new issues, solutions, and product updates.

In practice, organizations may blend elements from several of these methodologies to create a customized approach that works best for them. For instance, they might use ITIL's structure for overall service management, PDSA's cycle for continuous improvement initiatives, RACI matrices to define roles and responsibilities, COBIT's governance for alignment with business goals, and KCS^{SM} principles for knowledge management.

Conclusion

As we conclude this chapter on Go-Live and post-implementation support for Business Central, it's evident that the journey doesn't end at Go-Live. Rather, a new phase begins, one that is critical to the longevity and efficacy of the system. The post-implementation period is about nurturing the system to fulfill its intended purpose, ensuring that it grows with the organization, and continues to provide value.

We have dissected the structured methodologies and techniques that underpin successful post-implementation practices, including the importance of phased rollouts, the necessity of dry runs, the rigor of robust testing, the empowerment through user training, and the indispensability of support and communication channels. Moreover, the integration of methodologies such as ITIL and PDSA provides a framework for continuous improvement and operational excellence.

The true measure of success for a Business Central implementation is not just a flawless Go-Live but also how well the system is maintained and supported thereafter. The focus on continuous improvement, proactive support, and adaptive maintenance ensures that the system remains relevant, useful, and a strategic asset to the business.

As organizations navigate through the post-implementation landscape, the strategies and insights presented in this chapter will serve as a compass, guiding them toward a future where Business Central is not just a tool for today but a foundation for tomorrow's growth and innovation

KEY HIGHLIGHTS

- Careful preparation is essential for a successful Go-Live, with a focus on testing, user training, and data validation.

- A phased rollout approach can mitigate risks by allowing for smaller, manageable transitions and easier troubleshooting.

- Dry runs or dress rehearsals are crucial for uncovering and solving potential issues before the actual Go-Live.

- Comprehensive testing, including User Acceptance Testing (UAT), is necessary to ensure the system functions correctly and meets user needs.

- Effective user training and readily available documentation are key to helping users adapt to the new system.

- Strong support and clear communication channels during Go-Live are vital to address any immediate user concerns or technical issues.

- Active monitoring of system performance and establishing a feedback loop during Go-Live aid in rapid issue identification and resolution.

- Change management is a continuous process that requires attention beyond the Go-Live to secure user adoption and system optimization.

CHAPTER 11

Common Implementation Challenges and Solutions

Implementing Business Central, a dynamic enterprise resource planning system, is not just an undertaking but a transformative step toward operational excellence. This chapter shifts focus from traditional challenges to the remarkable advancements made by Microsoft in recent years.

Business Central now stands out with its extensive localization in 156 countries and support for 54 languages, positioning it as a top choice for global businesses. These developments are not static; every few months sees the addition of new countries and languages, further enhancing its appeal.

We'll explore how what were once hurdles have now become Business Central's strengths, encouraging you to conduct due diligence to ascertain how these features align with your specific needs. This chapter aims to provide insights that help turn potential obstacles into opportunities, illustrating why Business Central is a leading choice for businesses seeking a comprehensive, globally adaptable ERP solution.

© Dr. Gomathi S 2024
Dr. Gomathi S, *Mastering Microsoft Dynamics 365 Business Central*,
https://doi.org/10.1007/979-8-8688-0230-0_11

The objective is to provide you with the necessary knowledge to proactively identify and address common issues, thereby transforming potential obstacles into opportunities for achievement.

Overview

This chapter shifts the narrative from challenges to opportunities in the implementation of Business Central. It serves as a comprehensive guide, emphasizing the system's vast capabilities and global adaptability, making it accessible and beneficial for a diverse range of organizations.

Here, we explore pragmatic strategies derived from real-world applications and expert insights, focusing on how to tailor Business Central to unique business needs and seamlessly integrate it into existing workflows.

As you delve into this chapter, you'll gain a robust framework for harnessing Business Central's strengths, transforming potential challenges into opportunities for growth, and innovation. This is a journey toward not just implementing an ERP system, but embracing a tool that continuously evolves to meet global business demands.

Common Challenges

Recognizing prevalent obstacles encountered throughout the deployment of a system such as Business Central is an essential measure in guaranteeing a seamless transition and successful operations. Insights into the frequent obstacles that organizations frequently encounter during such implementations are provided below.

Comprehending Misalignments in Business Processes: An initial obstacle that arises is the incongruity between the current business procedures and the predefined functionalities provided by Business Central.

Frequently, established business procedures do not correspond precisely with the out-of-the-box solutions of the software.

Concerns Regarding Data Integrity and Migration

The process of migrating data from legacy systems to Business Central may give rise to challenges related to data integrity. It is critical to guarantee that data is precise, uncontaminated, and appropriately formatted in order to avert any disruptions to operations on the new system.

User Resistance to Change

Effective change management poses a substantial challenge. Employees who have become acclimated to a specific method of operation may exhibit resistance toward acquiring knowledge and adjusting to a novel system. Resistance may stem from apprehension toward the unfamiliar, apprehension regarding the intricacy involved, or unease regarding the modification of established processes.

Customizations

Addressing specific business requirements often necessitates customizations within Business Central. The challenge lies in ensuring these customizations are both effective and scalable, aligning with the growth and evolution of the business. Customizations should be planned meticulously to ensure they enhance, rather than complicate, the user experience and overall system performance.

Integrations

Integrating Business Central with existing legacy systems presents its own set of challenges. Often, the complexities stem more from these external systems than from Business Central itself. Ensuring seamless integration requires a comprehensive understanding of both the capabilities of Business Central and the technical specifications of the legacy systems. Successful integration is key to a unified and efficient operational ecosystem.

Budgetary and Temporal Limitations

Budget overruns and prolonged schedules may also present substantial obstacles. Implementations may incur greater expenses and consume more time than originally anticipated, resulting in discontent among stakeholders.

Ascertaining these obstacles constitutes the initial stage of the implementation process. This facilitates the development of focused resolutions and the creation of a well-defined course of action that acknowledges possible setbacks, thereby guaranteeing that the undertaking remains aligned with the intended results.

Other Challenges

Beyond the initial challenges already discussed, organizations implementing Business Central may encounter a variety of other hurdles, including

Regulatory Compliance and Security Concerns: Businesses must ensure that their new system complies with industry regulations and standards, which can vary widely depending on geography and sector.

Customization vs. Configuration Dilemma: Finding the balance between customizing the software to fit specific needs and using the available configuration options to adapt to the system's standard functionalities can be difficult. Over-customization can lead to increased costs and complexity.

Integration with Third-Party Applications: Many businesses use a range of software applications, and integrating these with Business Central can be complex. Ensuring seamless data flow between systems is crucial to maintain efficiency and accuracy.

Performance Optimization: Addressing performance optimization in Business Central, it's important to recognize the system's built-in scalability features. As businesses grow, Business Central adeptly handles increased demands through user license-based storage enhancements and the option for add-on storage. Each additional user license contributes not only to greater storage capacity but also to backend performance improvements. Furthermore, clients have the flexibility to purchase additional storage as needed, ensuring the system scales effectively with their business needs. This approach significantly reduces concerns about performance degradation even as transaction volumes and user loads grow.

Adapting to Continuous Updates: Unlike on-premises solutions, Business Central, especially in its cloud form, is updated regularly. Organizations must adapt to these updates, which can bring changes to functionality and require users to continuously adapt.

System Downtime and Maintenance: Addressing the aspects of system downtime and maintenance in the context of Business Central offers a more reassuring outlook than typically expected with ERP systems. Renowned for its exceptional uptime, Business Central boasts an impressive record of over 99.95% across all global regions. This remarkable level of reliability means that the challenges traditionally associated with system downtime and maintenance are significantly mitigated for businesses using Business Central, even for those operating 24/7.

This high uptime percentage ensures that the impact on daily operations is minimal, allowing businesses to plan for the rare instances of maintenance or updates with confidence. The robustness of Business Central in maintaining continuous operations can be a critical factor for businesses in their decision-making process, particularly for those requiring uninterrupted access to their ERP system. This aspect of Business Central's performance, detailed further at Business Central Status, highlights its suitability for businesses looking for a dependable, always-on solution.

Localization and Globalization: In the realm of localization and globalization, Business Central stands out for its wide-reaching capabilities. The software currently offers localization for 156 countries, a testament to its global applicability and adaptability. This expansive coverage means that businesses operating internationally can rely on Business Central to meet region-specific requirements. It's notable that localizations for countries not initially provided by Microsoft are often developed by top partners in the Business Central community. For instance, the localization for Sri Lanka was accomplished by my team, showcasing the collaborative and innovative nature of the Business Central ecosystem. Once these localizations are published by a top partner, they become available for other partners to utilize in their implementations, further extending the software's global footprint.

Regarding language support, Business Central is equally impressive, offering functionalities in 54 languages. This broad language support is largely contributed to by top partners, again illustrating the collaborative effort within the Business Central community to make the software as inclusive and accessible as possible. These features significantly ease the challenges of globalization and localization for businesses, ensuring that the software is not just a fit for their current operations but is also scalable to meet their future international expansion needs.

Solutions and Workarounds

Addressing the challenges of Business Central implementation involves strategic solutions and workarounds that mitigate risks and facilitate a smoother transition. Here are some solutions and workarounds for the challenges previously mentioned:

For Regulatory Compliance and Security Concerns:

- Utilize Business Central's compliance management features and regularly update security protocols.

- Work with compliance experts to tailor the system to meet specific regulatory requirements.

- Implement role-based access and data encryption to protect sensitive information.

For Complexity of Business Intelligence:

- Leverage Business Central's built-in analytics and reporting tools, and integrate them with Microsoft Power BI for advanced data visualization.

- Conduct thorough training sessions on analytics for users to fully understand and utilize these features.

For Customization vs. Configuration Dilemma:

For the Customization vs. Configuration Dilemma, three primary approaches can be considered:

- **Prioritize Configuration:**

  - Where possible, prefer configuring the existing features of Business Central over creating custom solutions. This approach minimizes complexity and eases future maintenance.

- **Meticulous Customization:**

  - If customization is necessary, it should be planned with precision. Ensure that these custom solutions are scalable and maintainable, aligning with long-term business goals.

- **Leverage Microsoft AppSource Applications:**

  - As a valuable third option, consider utilizing applications available on Microsoft AppSource that meet the required custom functionality. The significant business benefit of this approach is that these applications, being used by a broad client base, are continually improved and supported by their vendors. This ensures a higher standard of reliability and functionality. As previously discussed, including a link to AppSource provides easy access for readers seeking to explore this option further.

For Integration with Third-Party Applications:

- Use Business Central's APIs and existing connectors to integrate with third-party systems.

- Consider middleware solutions that can serve as a bridge between Business Central and other applications, ensuring data consistency.

For Performance Optimization:

- Monitor system performance regularly and adjust resources as needed.

- Work with Vendor support to understand best practices for scaling Business Central effectively.

For Adapting to Continuous Updates:

- Develop a process to review and test new updates in a controlled environment before rolling them out.

- Engage in continuous training and change management practices to keep users informed about new features and changes.

For System Downtime and Maintenance:

- Plan maintenance during off-peak hours to minimize impact on operations.

- Prepare backup processes to keep critical functions running during system unavailability.

For Localization and Globalization:

- Utilize Business Central's capabilities to support multiple languages and currencies.

- Work with local partners to understand regional requirements and incorporate them into the system.

General Workarounds:

- Develop a comprehensive project plan that includes risk assessment and mitigation strategies.

Promote user adoption by cultivating a culture of change and offering consistent training and support.

It is imperative to uphold transparent lines of communication with all stakeholders in order to effectively manage expectations and solicit feedback.

Often, the efficacy of these solutions is contingent on the particulars of a given business, such as its scale, sector, and operational intricacy. It is critical to approach every challenge by thoroughly comprehending the fundamental concerns and the ramifications that potential resolutions may have on the operations and objectives of the organization.

Adopting Business Central, or any enterprise resource planning (ERP) system, and overcoming its obstacles is a complex undertaking that demands strategic forethought, efficient communication, and a readiness to make adjustments. The following pragmatic advice will assist you in navigating these obstacles:

1. **Engage Stakeholders Early:**

   Ensure that the requirements and concerns of key stakeholders are addressed by involving them from the outset. This early participation can foster organization-wide support and buy-in.

2. **Emphasize User Training and Support:**

   Deliver all-encompassing training sessions that are customized to suit the specific responsibilities of each role within the organization. Ongoing support following implementation is essential in order to promptly attend to any concerns raised by users.

3. **Formulate Unambiguous Objectives and Metrics:**

   Define SMART objectives, which stand for specific, measurable, attainable, relevant, and time-bound, for the execution phase. Implement metrics to monitor progress and pinpoint areas that require improvement.

4. **Give Precedence to Data Quality:**

   Perform comprehensive data cleansing and preparation prior to migration in order to safeguard the integrity of data stored in Business Central.

5. **Execute Change Management Strategies:**

   Establish a methodical framework for overseeing the transition, encompassing communication strategies, training initiatives, and support systems to facilitate users' assimilation into the novel system.

6. **Opt for Incremental Implementation:**

   When deploying Business Central functionalities, contemplate a phased approach that commences with fundamental modules and progressively incorporates intricate features.

7. **Leverage the Power of Business Process Mapping:**

   Map current business processes to the new system to identify gaps and overlaps. This can help in understanding how Business Central can be configured to better align with organizational workflows.

8. **Stay Flexible and Adapt to Feedback:**

   Be prepared to iterate on your implementation plan based on feedback from users and performance data.

9. **Regularly Review and Optimize the System:**

   Post-implementation, regularly review the system's performance and user adoption, making adjustments as necessary to improve efficiency and satisfaction.

10. **Maintain Open Lines of Communication:**

    Encourage users to share their experiences and challenges. Regularly communicate updates, successes, and acknowledge the difficulties to maintain transparency.

11. **Plan for Ongoing Maintenance and Updates:**

    Schedule regular check-ins and updates to ensure the system remains efficient and secure.

12. **Seek Expert Assistance When Necessary:**

    Don't hesitate to consult with Business Central experts or partners for specialized knowledge and best practices.

By applying these tips, organizations can navigate the complexities of implementation, minimize disruptions, and enhance the chances of a successful Business Central deployment. Remember, the goal of implementation is not just to get the system up and running, but to do so in a way that adds value and supports the organization's strategic objectives.

Conclusion

In conclusion, the successful implementation of Business Central is a journey punctuated with challenges that demand attention, strategy, and agility. This chapter has equipped you with the foresight to identify common implementation challenges, the understanding to apply effective solutions and workarounds, and the practical tips to surmount the hurdles inherent in such a significant organizational change.

The key takeaway is that while the path to a fully functional Business Central environment is rarely without obstacles, these challenges are surmountable with careful planning, stakeholder engagement, and a commitment to continuous improvement. A focus on training, clear communication, and adherence to best practices can turn potential stumbling blocks into opportunities for optimization and growth.

It is crucial to bear in mind that the fundamental objective of integrating an enterprise resource planning (ERP) system such as Business Central is to enhance operational efficiency, acquire up-to-date information, and stimulate enterprise expansion. By adhering to the recommendations presented in this chapter, your organization will be in an advantageous position to effectively manage the intricacies of implementation and maximize the capabilities of Business Central.

As you move forward, keep in mind that implementation is not the end, but rather the beginning of a dynamic process of evolution and adaptation that, if managed well, will continuously yield returns on investment through improved efficiency, clarity, and decision-making capabilities.

KEY HIGHLIGHTS

- Understanding the importance of aligning Business Central implementation with existing business processes and addressing mismatches.

- Emphasizing the significance of clean data migration and strategies for maintaining data integrity.

- Recognizing user resistance as a natural part of the change process and employing change management techniques to ease the transition.

- Navigating technical challenges, including system integration and the necessity for customizations, with a balanced approach.

- Highlighting the need for comprehensive user training and ongoing support to ensure system adoption and proficiency.

- Addressing budgetary and time constraints through effective project management and realistic planning.

- Tackling regulatory compliance and data security concerns with rigorous protocols and stakeholder collaboration.

- Simplifying the complexities of leveraging Business Central's business intelligence and reporting tools for actionable insights.

- Strategizing the balance between necessary customizations and beneficial configurations to optimize system functionality.

- Ensuring seamless integration with third-party applications to maintain operational continuity.

- Planning for performance optimization to accommodate growth without compromising on system responsiveness.

- Preparing for continuous updates and maintenance with minimal disruption to business operations.

- Localizing and globalizing the system to meet the diverse needs of an international operation.

- Overcoming challenges through strategic planning, stakeholder engagement, and a culture of continuous improvement.

CHAPTER 12

Measuring Success and KPIs

A substantial financial commitment is required to implement an enterprise resource planning system such as Business Central in the ever-changing business environment. Fortunately, the organization will fully appreciate the value of this investment only when it is capable of precisely quantifying and understanding the outcomes of its execution. In this environment, key indicators of performance (KPIs) are critical.

KPIs, or key performance indicators, serve as navigational aids for businesses, offering quantitative values that highlight the company's progress toward operational and strategic goals. KPIs must be accurately specified in the context of Business Central implementation in order to reflect the organization's particular objectives and the system's capabilities.

The ability to measure success after deployment is not a one-time event, but rather a continuous process that demands continual examination and development. By staying focused on its goals, the organization may effectively adjust to changing circumstances in the market and internal dynamics.

© Dr. Gomathi S 2024
Dr. Gomathi S, *Mastering Microsoft Dynamics 365 Business Central*,
https://doi.org/10.1007/979-8-8688-0230-0_12

Overview

The intricacies of key performance indicators (KPIs) and its crucial significance in analyzing the efficacy of a Business Central deployment are examined in this chapter. In this talk, we will look at how to create relevant key performance indicators (KPIs) that correspond with your organization's goals, as well as how to use these metrics to draw practical conclusions. In addition, we will deliberate on the significance of continuous monitoring and enhancement, which guarantee that the performance of your Business Central system not only fulfills but surpasses anticipated levels over an extended period.

This chapter will provide business executives and project managers with the necessary understanding to establish impactful key performance indicators (KPIs) and utilize them to guide the success of their Business Central implementation.

Defining Key Performance Indicators (KPIs)

Determining Key Performance Indicators (KPIs) for Business Central necessitates a comprehensive comprehension of the system's functionalities and its congruence with the strategic goals of the organization. (SMART) KPIs ought to be the following: specific, measurable, achievable, relevant, and time-bound.[1] The subsequent is a structure for establishing KPIs within the framework of a Business Central implementation:

---

[1] www.atlassian.com/blog/productivity/how-to-write-smart-goals

1. **Financial Performance KPIs:**

   - **Profit Margins:** Monitoring profit margin fluctuations serves as an indicator of financial well-being.

   - **Cost Savings:** Assess the extent to which process automation contributes to decreases in operational expenses.

   - **Revenue Growth:** Observe revenue increases that transpire due to improved service or sales capabilities.

2. **Operational Efficiency KPIs:**

   - **Order Processing Time:** The time taken from order receipt to completion.

   - **Inventory Turnover:** How often inventory is sold and replaced over a period.

   - **Procurement Cycle Time:** The timeframe from raising a purchase order to receiving goods.

3. **Customer Engagement KPIs:**

   While Business Central is capable of measuring certain customer engagement KPIs like customer retention rates, it's the Dynamics 365 CRM/ Customer Service module that offers the specialized functionality needed to calculate and analyze CSAT and NPS. This distinction is crucial for businesses planning to leverage the full suite of Dynamics 365 tools to gain comprehensive insights into customer engagement and satisfaction.

- **Customer Retention Rates:** Percentage of customers who remain over a period.

- **Customer Satisfaction Score (CSAT):** A measure of how products or services meet customer expectations.

- **Net Promoter Score (NPS):** Gauges customer loyalty and the likelihood of referrals.

4. **Project-Specific KPIs (For Implementation Phase):**

   - **Implementation Budget Adherence:** The degree to which the implementation costs stay within budget.

   - **Milestone Completion Rate:** The percentage of project milestones completed on time.

   - **System Adoption Rate:** Proportion of staff actively using Business Central.

5. **Data and Analytics KPIs:**

   - **Report Accuracy:** The correctness of reports generated by Business Central.

   - **Data Entry Efficiency:** The time and effort required to input data into the system.

   - **Data Utilization:** The extent to which the data in Business Central is used for decision-making.

6. **Compliance and Security KPIs:**

- **Audit Trail Completeness:** The integrity and completeness of the audit logs within Business Central.

- **Access Control Violations:** Instances of unauthorized access attempts or policy violations.

KPI Example: Order Processing Time

1. **Objective:**

- **Definition:** To measure the efficiency of the order-to-fulfillment process.

- **Importance:** Shorter order processing times can lead to higher customer satisfaction and quicker inventory turnover, both of which are crucial for maintaining cash flow and customer loyalty.

2. **Formula:**

- **Calculation:** $(Sum of all individual order processing times)/(Total number of orders processed)$

- **Components:** This includes time from order entry to order fulfillment.

3. **Target:**

- **Goal:** Achieve an average order processing time of 24 hours.

- **Benchmarks:** Based on industry standards or historical data, this target may be adjusted to ensure it's challenging yet attainable.

4. **Data Source:**

   - **Primary Source:** Order processing module within Business Central.

   - **Validation:** Cross-reference with customer feedback and delivery times logged in shipping software if integrated.

5. **Reporting Frequency:**

   - **Review Period:** Weekly review for agile responsiveness, with monthly deep dives for trend analysis and strategy adjustments.

KPI Example: Customer Retention Rate

1. **Objective:**

   - **Definition:** To assess the percentage of customers who continue to do business over a given period.

   - **Importance:** High retention rates typically indicate customer satisfaction and loyalty, which are predictors of stable revenue and growth potential.

2. **Formula:**

   - **Calculation:**

     *(Numberofcustomersatendofperiod−
     Numberofnewcustomersduringtheperiod)/
     Numberofcustomersatstartofperiodx*100

   - **Components:** Customer counts over a specific period, excluding new customers to focus on retention

3. **Target:**

- **Goal:** Maintain a customer retention rate of 85% or above.

- **Benchmarks:** Set in relation to past performance and industry averages.

4. **Data Source:**

- **Primary Source:** Sales Module

- **Validation:** Surveys and follow-up engagement metrics

5. **Reporting Frequency:**

- **Review Period:** Quarterly for strategic planning and annual comparisons

KPI Example: Financial Accuracy

1. **Objective:**

- **Definition:** To gauge the precision of financial reporting and adherence to accounting standards.

- **Importance:** Accurate financial reports are essential for making informed business decisions and maintaining regulatory compliance.

2. **Formula:**

- **Calculation:** No standard formula; typically assessed through audit findings.

- **Components:** Number of discrepancies or adjustments required post-audit.

3. **Target:**

- **Goal:** Zero significant audit findings or adjustments.

- **Benchmarks:** Based on regulatory requirements and internal quality standards.

4. **Data Source:**

- **Primary Source:** Financial accounting module within Business Central.

- **Validation:** External audits and internal review mechanisms.

5. **Reporting Frequency:**

- **Review Period:** Annually in alignment with the fiscal year audit cycle.

Metrics for Evaluating Implementation Success

Metrics for evaluating the success of a Business Central implementation are critical indicators that provide insights into the effectiveness, efficiency, and business impact of the new ERP system. These metrics not only offer quantitative data on various aspects of the implementation but also enable organizations to make informed decisions about future investments and improvements.

When a company invests in an ERP system like Microsoft Dynamics 365 Business Central, it's essential to establish clear criteria for what success looks like. Success metrics serve as a quantifiable means to determine whether the implementation has achieved its intended goals.

Generally, these objectives concern the following: enhancing customer satisfaction, boosting employee productivity, and enhancing financial performance.

Why Metrics for Implementation Success Are Important

1. **Insights for Constant Enhancement:** Metrics furnish feedback regarding the effectiveness and inefficacy of an endeavor, facilitating the continuous enhancement of systems and processes.

2. **Objective Assessment:** They provide an impartial method for assessing the implementation, devoid of subjective viewpoints and predispositions.

3. **ROI Justification:** Success metrics are often tied to financial performance, helping justify the investment in the new system.

4. **Alignment with Business Goals:** They ensure that the implementation is aligned with strategic business objectives, not just IT goals.

5. **Stakeholder Confidence:** Clear metrics can build confidence among stakeholders by demonstrating tangible benefits.

Examples of Implementation Success Metrics

- **User Adoption Rates:** The percentage of employees using Business Central as part of their daily operations.

- **Solution Downtime:** The amount of time the system is unavailable or not functioning as expected.

- **Customer Satisfaction:** Changes in customer satisfaction levels post-implementation, which can be tracked through surveys or service metrics.

- **Data Quality:** The accuracy and reliability of data within Business Central, which can impact reporting and decision-making.

- **Budget Adherence:** Whether the implementation stayed within the allocated budget.

- **Time to Go Live:** The duration from project initiation to when Business Central is fully operational.

Case Study Application

Let's consider a fictional company, "ABC Manufacturing," that implemented Business Central. They set clear success metrics, including

- **Reduction in Order to Cash Cycle Time:** They wanted to decrease the time from when an order is placed to when payment is received. Post-implementation, ABC Manufacturing saw a 30% reduction in this cycle, exceeding their target of 20%.

- **Inventory Accuracy Improvement:** ABC Manufacturing aimed to improve inventory accuracy to reduce holding costs and lost sales due to stockouts. After Business Central was implemented, they reported a 25% improvement in inventory accuracy.

- **Increase in Financial Reporting Efficiency:** The company aimed to reduce the time taken to close monthly financials from 10 days to 5 days. After the implementation, they were able to close their books in 4 days, thereby achieving and surpassing their goal.

In this case study, the metrics not only showed that Business Central was successfully implemented but also revealed the system's positive impact on the company's operational efficiency and financial performance. By comparing pre- and post-implementation figures, ABC Manufacturing could quantify the success of their ERP project.

In conclusion, defining and tracking the right metrics is vital for any Business Central implementation. It's these metrics that provide the factual basis for evaluating the project's success and guiding future enhancements, ensuring that the system delivers value to the business on an ongoing basis.

Monitoring and Continuous Improvements

Monitoring and continuous improvement are integral to maintaining and enhancing the value of a Business Central implementation over time. This involves ongoing tracking of performance, systematic evaluation, and the iterative refinement of business processes and system functionality.

Monitoring:

Monitoring in the context of Business Central involves the regular collection and analysis of data to assess performance against the defined KPIs. Real-time dashboards and reporting features within Business Central, and Power BI integration, allow for continuous monitoring of various metrics.

Continuous Improvement

Continuous improvement is about taking the insights gained from
monitoring and using them to make incremental changes that lead to
better efficiency, higher user satisfaction, and greater ROI. The concept
is rooted in various business management philosophies, such as Kaizen,
which emphasizes small, continuous positive changes that improve
productivity and efficiency.

Specific Methods for Monitoring and Continuous Improvement

PDCA (Plan-Do-Check-Act) Cycle[2]:

- **Plan:** Identify areas for improvement, define objectives,
  and plan actions.

- **Do:** Implement the planned changes on a small
  scale first.

- **Check:** Monitor the results and compare them against
  the expected outcomes.

- **Act:** If the change was successful, implement it on
  a wider scale. If not, begin the cycle again with a
  different plan.

---

[2] www.mindtools.com/as2l5i1/pdca-plan-do-check-act

Six Sigma[3]:

- Utilizes five phases (Define, Measure, Analyze, Improve, and Control) to improve processes by identifying and removing the causes of defects

Total Quality Management (TQM)[4]:

- A management approach centered on quality, based on the participation of all members of an organization in improving processes, products, services, and the culture in which they work.

Models for Continuous Improvement

KPI-Driven Model:

- This model relies on the consistent measurement of KPIs to identify areas for improvement. When a KPI does not meet the set target, it triggers a review and improvement process.

User Feedback Model:

- Regular user feedback is solicited and analyzed to identify system issues and areas for enhancement. This model ensures the system evolves in line with user needs.

---

[3] https://en.wikipedia.org/wiki/Six_Sigma
www.investopedia.com/terms/t/total-quality-management-tqm.
asp#:~:text=TQM%20is%20considered%20a%20customer,are%20in%20place%20
for%20production

[4] www.atlassian.com/blog/productivity/how-to-write-smart-goals

Agile/Scrum Methodology:

- Although traditionally used in software development, Agile principles can apply to ERP system improvements, with iterative development and frequent reassessment.

ITIL Service Management:

- Focused on aligning IT services with the needs of the business, ITIL provides a framework for managing IT as a service and for continuous service improvement.

For effective monitoring and continuous improvement, organizations should

- Establish a routine schedule for reviewing KPIs and system performance.

- Encourage feedback from all system users and stakeholders.

- Prioritize improvements based on strategic impact and feasibility.

- Leverage Business Central updates and customization capabilities to adapt to changing needs.

- Keep abreast of new features and best practices in the ERP community that could enhance system usage.

By employing these methods and models, businesses can ensure that their Business Central implementation remains effective, efficient, and aligned with evolving business objectives. It is an ongoing process that requires commitment from all levels of the organization, from end users to top management.

Let's delve into each of the continuous improvement methods with examples, particularly as they might apply to monitoring and enhancing a Microsoft Dynamics 365 Business Central implementation.

PDCA (Plan-Do-Check-Act) Cycle:

Example: Suppose a company using Business Central identifies that the month-end closing process is taking too long, which delays financial reporting.

- **Plan**: The finance team plans to automate certain entries that are currently manual and create a new workflow within Business Central to streamline the process.

- **Do**: They implement the new automated entries and workflow on a small scale for one business unit.

- **Check**: After the first month-end close, they measure the time taken and compare it with previous months.

- **Act**: Seeing a significant reduction in time, they roll out the new workflow to all business units. If there wasn't an improvement, they would reassess and modify the plan.

Six Sigma:

Example: A retail company notices inconsistencies in inventory data within Business Central, leading to stockouts and overstocking.

- **Define**: The project's scope is defined to improve inventory accuracy.

- **Measure**: Current inventory accuracy rates are measured to establish a baseline.

- **Analyze**: The team analyzes inventory processes to identify causes of inaccuracies, such as data entry errors or timing delays in updates.

- **Improve**: Solutions like barcode scanning for inventory entries and real-time data synchronization are implemented.

- **Control**: New standard operating procedures are documented, and inventory accuracy is continually monitored to ensure improvements are sustained.

Total Quality Management (TQM):

Example: A manufacturing firm aims to improve the quality of its products by reducing the defect rate reported through Business Central's quality control module.

- The entire company, from executives to production line workers, is engaged in a culture of quality improvement.

- Cross-functional teams are formed to review quality control data and suggest improvements.

- Quality improvement becomes a company-wide KPI, with regular meetings to discuss progress and share best practices.

- As a result, the defect rate decreases, and customer satisfaction scores improve.

KPI-Driven Model:

Example: A service company is experiencing delays in service delivery, and the KPI of "Average Time to Service Completion" is not meeting targets.

- They continuously monitor this KPI through Business Central's service management dashboard.

- When the KPI shows a consistent failure to meet the target, a task force is convened to address the issue.

- The task force identifies bottlenecks in the service process and implements changes.

- As the KPI begins to improve, the team establishes new benchmarks to strive for further improvements.

User Feedback Model:

Example: End users of Business Central in a distribution company find the sales order entry process cumbersome and slow.

- A feedback loop is established where users can report issues or suggestions.

- Analysis of feedback indicates that the user interface could be more intuitive.

- The company customizes the sales order entry screen based on user suggestions.

- User satisfaction with the system increases, as reflected in subsequent feedback.

Agile/Scrum Methodology:

Example: A company wants to continuously enhance their Business Central system to keep up with evolving business requirements.

- They adopt an Agile approach, breaking down the enhancement process into two-week sprints.

- Each sprint focuses on a specific set of improvements, such as adding a new feature or refining an existing module.

- The team reviews progress at the end of each sprint, prioritizing tasks for the next one.

- This iterative process allows for rapid and responsive system enhancements.

ITIL Service Management:

Example: An organization wants to ensure that their Business Central system is reliable and consistently meets the needs of the business.

- They adopt ITIL practices to manage Business Central as a service.

- They set up a service desk within Business Central to handle user issues and requests.

- Regular service reviews are conducted to discuss performance against service level agreements (SLAs).

- Continuous service improvement is part of the routine, with changes made based on service review outcomes and metrics.

In each of these examples, the core principles of continuous improvement—measurement, evaluation, and incremental change—are used to refine and optimize the use of Business Central. These methods foster an environment of excellence and adaptability, ensuring that the system continues to support the organization's goals effectively.

Table 12-1. *Method Summary*

Method	Responsible Party
PDCA Cycle	Process Owners, Quality Assurance Teams, Management
Six Sigma	Six Sigma Black Belts/Green Belts, Process Improvement Teams
Total Quality Management (TQM)	All Employees, Led by TQM Coordinators or Quality Managers
KPI-Driven Model	Department Heads, KPI Owners, Business Analysts
User Feedback Model	Customer Service Managers, Product Owners, UX/UI Teams
Agile/Scrum Methodology	Scrum Master, Product Owner, Agile Teams
ITIL Service Management	IT Service Managers, ITIL Practitioners, Service Desk Teams

Conclusion

We reflect on the pivotal role that well-defined metrics play in not only capturing the immediate outcomes of the implementation but also in steering long-term success and continuous improvement.

Through the meticulous definition of KPIs, we've seen how quantifiable measures can bring clarity and focus to the evaluation process, allowing businesses to gauge whether their new system is in harmony with their strategic goals. Whether it's through the lens of financial performance, operational efficiency, customer satisfaction, or data quality, KPIs act as the beacon that guides the ship of Business Central implementation toward the shores of success.

We delved into specific methods such as PDCA, Six Sigma, and TQM, which provide structured approaches to ongoing improvement. In conjunction with the KPI-driven approach, input from customers, Agile principles, and ITIL service management, these methodologies constitute a comprehensive framework that enables organizations to not only oversee their Business Central environment but also enhance it on an ongoing basis. Every approach offers a distinct viewpoint regarding enhancement, guaranteeing that the system adapts to accommodate the dynamic requirements of the organization and its clientele.

The objective of this chapter was to furnish you with the requisite understanding and resources to delineate, assess, and enhance your Business Central implementation. The progression from the initial implementation to the complete utilization of Business Central is ongoing and ever-changing. It is a voyage characterized by growth, adaptation, and learning.

In summary, it is crucial to bear in mind that the true efficacy of Business Central is not solely derived from its extensive functionalities, but rather from its seamless integration with organizational procedures, the proficient integration of your team, and the ongoing refinement to align with the perpetually evolving business environment. Your dedication to evaluating progress and pursuing enhancement is what will ultimately determine the worth that Business Central contributes to your organization.

KEY HIGHLIGHTS

- Defining KPIs that align with business goals is crucial for evaluating the success of a Business Central implementation.

- Specialized metrics such as system adoption rates, process efficiency gains, and customer satisfaction levels provide insight into the implementation's effectiveness.

- Financial KPIs including cost savings, revenue growth, and ROI are essential for justifying the investment in Business Central.

- Monitoring KPIs through tools like Power BI integrated with Business Central enables real-time performance tracking.

- Continuous improvement methodologies such as PDCA, Six Sigma, and TQM help organizations iteratively enhance their Business Central usage.

- Each role within the organization, from executives to end users, has specific responsibilities for ensuring the success of Business Central implementation.

- Regular review and refinement of KPIs ensure that Business Central continues to meet the evolving needs of the business.

- A culture of continuous improvement and data-driven decision-making supports the long-term success of Business Central within an organization.

CHAPTER 13

Future Trends in ERP and Business Central

As we embark on a journey through the evolving landscape of enterprise resource planning (ERP), it is crucial to recognize the tangible benefits these advancements bring to organizations. In this chapter, we will explore the future trends in ERP and specifically in Microsoft Dynamics 365 Business Central, not just from a technological standpoint but through the lens of functional enhancements that drive organizational value.

The advent of new modules and extensions tailored to various vertical industries signifies a leap in application capabilities. These enhancements are not merely technical upgrades; they represent a deeper alignment with specific industry needs, enabling organizations to leverage ERP solutions more effectively in their unique operational contexts.

The integration of Microsoft's Power Platform with Business Central is a testament to the ERP system's adaptability. This extension capability allows organizations to customize and extend their ERP solutions rapidly, ensuring they can keep pace with the ever-changing business environment.

Artificial Intelligence (AI) is no longer a futuristic concept but a present reality in ERP systems. The infusion of AI, including features like Copilot and other AI innovations, transforms data into actionable insights,

© Dr. Gomathi S 2024
Dr. Gomathi S, *Mastering Microsoft Dynamics 365 Business Central*,
https://doi.org/10.1007/979-8-8688-0230-0_13

automates routine tasks, and enhances decision-making processes. This AI integration is not just about technological sophistication; it's about empowering organizations to be more proactive and data-driven.

The global availability of Business Central, encompassing various countries, regions, and languages, breaks down geographical and linguistic barriers. This expansion ensures that organizations around the world can access an ERP solution that speaks their language and understands their regional nuances.

User experience enhancements in ERP systems are pivotal in driving productivity. By making these systems more intuitive and user-friendly, organizations can ensure higher adoption rates, reduced training times, and ultimately, enhanced productivity.

Governance and administration features within ERP systems are evolving to provide better control and oversight. This evolution is crucial for organizations to maintain robust data governance and operational integrity.

Legislation compliance is a critical aspect of ERP systems. As laws and regulations change, ERP systems must adapt to ensure organizations remain compliant, thereby mitigating legal risks and maintaining operational legitimacy.

Reporting and data analysis capabilities within ERP systems are becoming more advanced, turning vast amounts of data into meaningful insights. This enhancement is crucial for organizations to understand their performance, identify trends, and make informed strategic decisions.

Lastly, the service and platform enhancements, including considerations for availability, Business Continuity Planning (BCP), and Disaster Recovery (DR), ensure that organizations can rely on their ERP systems in all circumstances. These enhancements are about building resilience and ensuring uninterrupted operations.

In this chapter, we will delve into each of these aspects, connecting them to the foundational knowledge addressed in the previous chapters of this book. Our goal is to provide a cohesive understanding of how these future trends in ERP and Business Central will bring about transformative benefits to organizations across various industries.

Overview

The goal of this chapter is to give you a full picture of where ERP systems are going in the future by focusing on new ideas and trends that will change how businesses work. First, we'll look at the new trends in ERP, pick out the most important technology advances, and talk about what these mean for businesses of all sizes. We will look into how these developments are affecting ERP plans and the way decisions are made as part of this investigation.

The second topic up for discussion is Microsoft's excellent ERP system, Dynamics 365 Business Central. Business Central's future features will be examined to determine how the platform can adapt to an ever-evolving environment. This portion would not only address the fresh capabilities and functions which will be added to Business Central, yet it will also talk about how these improvements fit in with the wider trends in the ERP business.

This chapter will not only discuss these issues, but will also provide examples and case studies of their application and impact on actual businesses. The purpose of this chapter is to foretell what the future holds in terms of ERP and Business Central so that readers can not only prepare for, but also take advantage of, these developments.

This chapter will not only reveal what lies ahead for ERP systems, but it will also provide insight into how businesses may adapt to the rapidly evolving digital landscape.

Emerging Trends in ERP

The ever-evolving nature of both technology and business requirements is reflected in the latest ERP developments. The following developments were significantly altering the ERP landscape:

Cloud-Based ERP

One of the most consequential shifts is the increasing use of cloud-based ERP solutions. When compared to conventional, on-premises systems, these alternatives excel in flexibility, scalability, and efficiency. They also facilitate remote data access, which is crucial in today's increasingly mobile and decentralized workplaces.

Artificial intelligence (AI) and machine learning (ML) are increasingly being integrated into enterprise resource planning (ERP) software. This integration makes it possible to evaluate data more intelligently, generate predictions, and automate mundane operations. Artificial intelligence can aid with forward planning, inventory management, and providing a more customized experience for each individual consumer. The outcome is an enterprise resource planning system that is both upbeat and operative.

Business Intelligence

Modern enterprise resource planning systems offer users effective analytics and business intelligence features, allowing them to obtain a better understanding of their companies' inner workings. This trend enables firms to make data-driven decisions, identify trends, and identify areas where their procedures aren't performing as well as they should.

Introducing the Internet of Things (IoT)

Once IoT is integrated with ERP systems, it enables real-time data collection and analysis. Because IoT devices can monitor and enhance the performance of physical assets, this integration is especially valuable in manufacturing, shipping, and supply chain management.

Mobile Accessibility

The growing need for mobile access to ERP systems demonstrates the requirement for employees to be able to operate from home or on the go. Mobile-friendly ERP solutions enable users to obtain data, make choices, and collaborate in real-time from any location, increasing total productivity.

Improvements to the User Experience and Usability

The user experience and layout of ERP systems are getting more and more attention. Standard features like personalized dashboards, user-friendly designs, and easy-to-understand interfaces are meant to boost usage and make it easier for new users to get started.

Security and Compliance

Companies have to follow more rules; ERP systems are changing to provide better tools for managing compliance. With the number of cyber dangers growing, better security features are also becoming an important part of ERP systems.

Ethics and Social Accountability

ERP systems now include features for managing social and environmental impacts, such as sustainability metrics and ethical supply chain management. A key point to note is that cloud-based ERPs generally have a lower carbon footprint compared to on-premise systems. This is due to the more efficient resource utilization in cloud data centers, which leads to reduced energy consumption and lower overall emissions. By opting for cloud ERPs, businesses not only embrace technological efficiency but also contribute to environmental sustainability.

Customization and Flexibility

More customization and flexibility are available in modern ERP systems to meet the needs of a wider range of businesses and industries. Moving away from the "one size fits all" method, this trend lets businesses change their ERP solutions to fit their specific needs and ways of doing things.

Adding Collaboration Tools

Adding collaboration tools to ERP systems is becoming more and more popular. This integration makes it easier for teams to talk to each other and work together, which improves project management and workflow.

These trends show that ERP solutions are becoming smarter, more flexible, and more focused on the user. These solutions will be able to adapt to the changing needs of modern businesses. The way businesses run their businesses and make strategic choices will change in the future because of these trends.

Future Innovation and Trends in Business Central

Dynamics 365 Business Central from Microsoft had long been a strong and flexible ERP system. Looking into the future, we can anticipate several innovations that could further enhance its capabilities and align it with emerging business needs and technological advancements. Here are some potential future innovations for Business Central:

Deeper Integration with AI and Machine Learning

Business Central could expand its AI capabilities for predictive analytics, offering more advanced forecasting, personalized customer insights, and intelligent automation of business processes. This could include AI-driven financial insights and inventory optimization.

Example:

Microsoft Dynamics 365 Business Central, enhanced with Microsoft Copilot, is revolutionizing business operations with its AI capabilities. For instance, Copilot significantly speeds up and improves the accuracy of bank account reconciliations, transforming a traditionally time-consuming task into an efficient process. In marketing, it assists in generating creative text suggestions, aiding in the development of effective communication strategies. The AI integration extends to inventory management as well, where it predicts future inventory needs based on sales trends, helping businesses optimize stock levels and reduce waste. Additionally, in financial management, Business Central uses past payment patterns of customers to forecast receivables, providing businesses with more accurate cash flow predictions, which is essential for effective financial planning and liquidity management. These examples highlight the diverse and practical benefits of AI integration in Business Central, enhancing various aspects of business operations from finance to marketing.

Enhanced IoT Capabilities

Integrating more deeply with the Internet of Things (IoT) could allow Business Central to offer real-time monitoring and management of business operations. This would be particularly beneficial in sectors like manufacturing, logistics, and retail, where IoT can provide immediate data on supply chains, production lines, and inventory levels.

For **example**, in factories, IoT devices could send data to Business Central in real time to keep an eye on how well equipment is working. Business Central could automatically plan maintenance, order replacement parts, or change production schedules if a machine starts to work in ways that aren't optimal.

Combining Augmented Reality (AR) and Virtual Reality (VR)

AR and VR can be used to create realistic data visualizations, train people, and help people from afar. For instance, in a manufacturing setting, AR could help people see how to do maintenance or production jobs by connecting directly to Business Central's data.

For example, AR could be used to make complicated data in Business Central easier to understand. For instance, a logistics business could use AR to see the logistics of the supply chain in 3D, which would help them find problems or areas where things aren't working as well as they could.

Blockchain Integration

Adding blockchain technology to Business Central could make it safer, more open, and easier to track. This could be very helpful for managing the supply chain because it would make sure that goods are tracked safely and clearly from where they are made to where they are sold.

Example: For a company managing a supply chain, blockchain could be used to record transactions in Business Central, ensuring traceability and transparency. Each product's journey from manufacturer to end user could be securely logged, providing undeniable proof of origin and handling.

Advanced Customization and App Development

Future versions of Business Central might offer even more advanced tools for customization and app development, allowing businesses to tailor the ERP system more precisely to their specific needs without extensive coding.

Example: Business Central could offer a platform where businesses can develop custom apps without extensive coding knowledge. For example, a bespoke app could be created for a unique inventory management need, seamlessly integrating with the core Business Central system.

Improved Collaboration Tools: Enhanced integration with collaboration platforms like Microsoft Teams, along with built-in communication tools, could facilitate better teamwork and decision-making directly within the ERP environment.

Example: Integrating with tools like Microsoft Teams, Business Central could allow a project team to discuss budget reports or project timelines directly within the ERP system, streamlining communication and decision-making processes.

Sustainability Management Features: As businesses increasingly focus on sustainability, Business Central could include features to track and manage a company's environmental impact, helping businesses achieve their sustainability goals.

Example: Business Central could help companies track their carbon footprint or waste management. For instance, it could analyze energy consumption data across different departments, helping businesses identify areas where they can reduce their environmental impact.

Greater Emphasis on User Experience and Accessibility: Future iterations might focus more on user experience, offering a more intuitive interface, personalized dashboards, and enhanced accessibility features to cater to a diverse range of users.

Example: Future versions might feature a more intuitive interface with customizable dashboards tailored to individual roles. For example, a financial controller might have a dashboard specifically designed to highlight key financial metrics and alerts.

Robust Data Privacy and Security: With increasing concerns about data privacy and security, Business Central could incorporate more advanced security protocols and compliance tools to protect sensitive business data and adhere to global data protection regulations.

Hybrid Cloud Solutions: While Business Central is primarily cloud-based, future innovations might include more flexible hybrid solutions that allow businesses to store some data on-premises while leveraging the cloud for other functionalities.

These potential innovations would not only enhance the functionality of Business Central but also ensure that it remains at the forefront of ERP technology, catering to the evolving needs of modern businesses.

Conclusion

The future of ERP systems, particularly Microsoft Dynamics 365 Business Central, is poised for transformative growth, driven by technological advancements and evolving business needs. The integration of AI, enhanced data analytics, IoT, and other emerging technologies will not only streamline business processes but also offer deeper insights and improved decision-making capabilities. As these systems become more adaptable, user-friendly, and environmentally conscious, they will play a crucial role in shaping the operational efficiency and strategic direction of organizations across various industries. This evolution of ERP systems signifies a new era of digital empowerment for businesses, ready to navigate the complexities of a rapidly changing global market.

KEY HIGHLIGHTS

- Transitioning from traditional systems to more flexible, cloud-based ERP solutions

- Integrating AI and machine learning for predictive analytics and smarter decision-making

- Incorporating advanced data analytics for deeper business insights

- Utilizing IoT for real-time data collection and analysis in sectors like manufacturing and logistics

- Emphasizing mobile accessibility for on-the-go data access and decision-making

- Enhancing user experience with user-friendly interfaces and personalized experiences

- Strengthening data security and compliance features in ERP systems.

- Moving toward customizable and flexible ERP solutions to meet specific business needs

- Predicting future advancements in Business Central, including AI, blockchain technology, and sustainability features

CHAPTER 14

Conclusion

As we near the conclusion of this comprehensive exploration of the complexities associated with the implementation of Microsoft Dynamics 365 Business Central, it is imperative to pause and contemplate the terrain that has been covered. The entire process, commencing with the fundamental stages of pre-implementation planning and progressing steadily through vendor selection, project management, and data migration, has been a critical component in the development of a resilient and robust enterprise resource planning (ERP) system.

We have thoroughly examined the functional and technical aspects of Business Central, uncovering its capacity to fundamentally transform business processes. By disseminating knowledge via practical case studies, optimal approaches, and strategic considerations, a road map has been established to effectively navigate the obstacles and optimize the worth of the system.

Change management, user adoption, and integration, the pillars of successful implementation, attest to the significance of human factors in conjunction with technological excellence. Placing emphasis on testing, quality assurance, and post-implementation support signifies that the process does not culminate in the successful launch of the system, but rather transforms into an ongoing pursuit of excellence.

© Dr. Gomathi S 2024
Dr. Gomathi S, *Mastering Microsoft Dynamics 365 Business Central,*
https://doi.org/10.1007/979-8-8688-0230-0_14

Regarding strategic objectives and progress monitoring, the discourse surrounding key performance indicators (KPIs) and success metrics serves as a guiding principle for organizations. The guidance on data purification and migration ensures that organizations can place their trust in the critical asset of their operations—their data—in a world where data is of the utmost importance.

Anticipating the future, the course of enterprise resource planning (ERP) systems is dynamic, as forthcoming advancements hold the potential to further augment Business Central. Organizations' competitive advantage will be determined by their capacity to swiftly adjust to these emerging trends.

In the rapidly evolving realm of enterprise resource planning, the roles of Artificial Intelligence (AI) and Business Intelligence (BI) are becoming increasingly pivotal. These technologies, when integrated with Business Central, unlock unprecedented levels of analytical power and automation capabilities. AI enhances the system's ability to predict trends, automate routine tasks, and provide insightful recommendations, thereby augmenting decision-making processes.

Concurrently, BI transforms vast amounts of data into actionable intelligence, offering a clearer view of business performance and customer insights. This symbiosis of AI and BI within Business Central not only streamlines operations but also fosters a more proactive and data-driven business culture. As organizations adapt to these advanced technologies, they position themselves at the forefront of innovation, ensuring that their Business Central implementation remains cutting-edge and fully leverages the potential of digital transformation.

Recall, as the reader, that the integration of Business Central into your organization signifies more than a mere undertaking; rather, it is an odyssey of profound change. This situation presents a prospect to optimize processes, enable personnel to advance, and redefine the way in which customers interact with the organization. Equipped with this manual, you are presently capable of traversing this expedition with assurance and accuracy.

Peruse the checklists provided in the annexures as a guiding companion and compass as you venture into the forthcoming digital environment of your organization. In addition to the technology itself, the achievement of success with your Business Central implementation is contingent upon your strategic foresight and scrupulous execution.

APPENDIX A

Assessing Business Needs and Requirement Gathering

This checklist serves as a systematic guide for the critical process of gathering requirements before implementing Microsoft Dynamics 365 Business Central. Through a comprehensive business analysis, stakeholders' engagement, and the definition of SMART objectives, the checklist ensures a clear understanding of the organization's needs.

Utilizing tools, collaboration platforms, and assessing cross-departmental dependencies, the checklist facilitates a holistic understanding of the current state. Recognizing requirements, pinpointing pain points, evaluating risks, addressing customization demands, ensuring the solution's future resilience, and considering user training are all essential elements of a comprehensive pre-implementation strategy. Documentation, feedback mechanisms, and alignment with Business

© Dr. Gomathi S 2024
Dr. Gomathi S, *Mastering Microsoft Dynamics 365 Business Central*,
https://doi.org/10.1007/979-8-8688-0230-0

Central capabilities are integral aspects, ensuring a well-informed and strategic approach to requirements gathering. This annexure is a valuable resource for project teams aiming for a successful and tailored implementation journey.

1. **Comprehensive Business Analysis:**

   - **Current State Analysis:**

     - Document existing business processes thoroughly.

     - Record details about the current state of systems and applications in use.

     - Identify bottlenecks, inefficiencies, and redundancies in current processes.

     - Document the OD, Database version, data flow, and dependencies between different departments.

   - **Areas for Improvement:**

     - Identify pain points and challenges in the current processes.

     - Explore opportunities for process optimization.

     - Consider feedback from end users regarding current difficulties.

     - Evaluate the usability of existing systems and interfaces.

2. **Stakeholder Engagement:**

   - **Departmental Representatives:**

     - Engage with representatives from each department, including finance, operations, sales, and others.

- Conduct interviews or surveys to gather insights from different teams.

- Identify key stakeholders who will be directly impacted by the implementation.

- **User Feedback:**

  - Gather feedback from end users on current system limitations.

  - Understand user preferences and pain points in day-to-day tasks.

  - Consider holding workshops or focus groups to encourage open communication.

  - Identify power users who can provide valuable insights.

3. **SMART Objectives Definition:**

   - **Specific Objectives:**

     - Clearly define the specific goals of the implementation.

     - Ensure that each objective addresses a specific business need.

     - Align objectives with the overall strategic vision of the organization.

   - **Measurable Objectives:**

     - Define metrics to measure the success of each objective.

     - Quantify improvement goals where possible.

     - Ensure that progress can be tracked and evaluated objectively.

- **Achievable Objectives:**

  - Assess the feasibility of each objective within resource constraints.

  - Consider the organization's capacity for change.

  - Ensure that objectives are realistic and attainable.

- **Relevant Objectives:**

  - Align each objective with the broader business strategy.

  - Ensure that each objective contributes directly to organizational success.

  - Confirm that objectives address the identified pain points.

- **Time-Bound Objectives:**

  - Define specific timelines for achieving each objective.

  - Consider the dependencies between different objectives.

  - Establish deadlines for key milestones.

4. **Tools and Templates Utilization:**

- **Business Analysis Tools:**

  - Utilize tools for process mapping and analysis.

  - Explore software solutions for data gathering and requirements documentation.

  - Implement templates for consistency in data collection and analysis.

- **Collaboration Tools:**
    - Use collaborative platforms for stakeholder engagement.
    - Employ tools that facilitate real-time collaboration among team members.
    - Choose tools that allow for version control and traceability.

5. **Holistic Understanding:**

- **Cross-Departmental Dependencies:**
    - Identify dependencies between different departments.
    - Understand how changes in one area may impact others.
    - Document interdepartmental workflows and data exchanges.

- **Integration Points:**
    - Identify existing integrations with external systems.
    - Document data exchange points with third-party applications.
    - Assess the impact of changes on integration points.
    - Identify the new integration points with Business Central.

- Identify the integration technology for each system. For example, API (preferred) File Bases such as SCV or XM, etc.

- Current system vendor capability to integrate the solution if needed.

6. **Requirement Gathering:**

- **User Interviews:**

  - Conduct one-on-one interviews with end users.

  - Encourage users to express challenges they face in their daily tasks.

  - Document specific pain points raised by different user groups.

- **Surveys and Feedback Forms:**

  - Distribute surveys to collect anonymous feedback.

  - Use feedback forms during workshops or training sessions.

  - Analyze trends in the feedback to identify common pain points.

7. **Risk Assessment:**

- **Risk Identification:**

  - Identify potential risks associated with the current state.

  - Evaluate risks related to the proposed changes.

  - Consider both technical and organizational risks.

- **Risk Mitigation Strategies:**
  - Develop strategies to mitigate identified risks.
  - Assign responsibilities for risk mitigation actions.
  - Establish contingency plans for high-impact risks.

8. **Customization and Configuration Requirements:**
   - **Module Customization:**
     - Identify modules that require customization.
     - Document specific functionalities that need adjustment.
     - Consider the impact of customization on user experience.
   - **Data Configuration:**
     - Assess data configuration needs based on business requirements.
     - Identify data fields that require customization.
     - Consider data migration requirements for existing records.

9. **User Training Needs:**
   - **Skills Assessment:**
     - Evaluate the skill levels of end users.
     - Identify areas where additional training is required.
     - Assess familiarity with the new system's interface.

- **Assess the Quality and Completeness of the Training Material and Training Process:**
  - Develop training materials tailored to user needs.
  - Create guides, tutorials, and documentation.
  - Consider interactive training sessions for hands-on learning.

10. **Documentation:**

- **Requirements Documentation:**
  - Document all gathered requirements in a structured manner.
  - Include detailed descriptions of each requirement.
  - Maintain version control for ongoing updates.

- **Assess the Quality and Completeness of the User Guides:**
  - Create user guides for the new system.
  - Ensure that guides are accessible and easy to understand.
  - Include step-by-step instructions for common tasks.

11. **Feedback Mechanism:**

- **Continuous Communication:**
  - Establish channels for continuous feedback.

- Encourage stakeholders to provide ongoing input.

- Regularly review and respond to feedback.

- **Adjustment Iterations:**

  - Plan for iterations based on feedback.

  - Adjust requirements and plans as needed.

  - Communicate changes transparently with stakeholders.

12. **Alignment with Business Central Capabilities:**

- **Feature Evaluation:**

  - Evaluate the features and capabilities of Business Central.

  - Confirm that identified requirements align with the system's capabilities.

  - Consider potential additional features offered by the platform.

  - Consider upcoming major features.

- **Vendor Consultation:**

  - Consult with Microsoft Dynamics 365 Business Central experts or vendor representatives.

  - Seek guidance on the feasibility of specific requirements.

  - Leverage vendor expertise for optimal system utilization.

APPENDIX B

Sample Interview Questions

Before beginning the role-play interview, take some time to prepare. Review the scenario description and the sample interview questions. Consider the role you will play as the decision-maker and how you will evaluate the vendor representative's responses.

During the interview, focus on actively engaging with the vendor representative, asking relevant questions, and assessing their alignment with your organization's goals and values. Practice effective communication and collaboration skills throughout the interaction.

1. **Vendor Background and Experience**:

    - Can you provide an overview of your company's experience in implementing Microsoft Dynamics 365 Business Central?

    - Have you worked with organizations similar to ours in terms of industry and size?

    - Vendor Staff Certifications: How many have been certified with MB800?

    - Vendor competency certification by Microsoft, which is Business Applications Solution Partner.

© Dr. Gomathi S 2024
Dr. Gomathi S, *Mastering Microsoft Dynamics 365 Business Central*,
https://doi.org/10.1007/979-8-8688-0230-0

- Vendor award from Microsoft such as Biz Apps Partner of the year.

- Apps published by the vendor on Microsoft AppSource.

- Experience in implementing Business Central in Overseas markets.

2. **Alignment with Objectives**:

   - How do you typically approach understanding a client's specific objectives for an implementation project?

   - Can you share examples of how you've aligned your services with a client's unique project goals in the past?

3. **Communication and Collaboration**:

   - Describe your approach to communication during an implementation project. How do you keep clients informed about progress and challenges?

   - How do you encourage collaboration between your team and the client's team to ensure project success?

4. **Customization and Tailoring**:

   - How do you approach customizing the Microsoft Dynamics 365 Business Central solution to meet a client's specific needs and business processes?

   - Can you provide examples of how you've tailored solutions for clients with unique requirements?

5. **Problem-Solving and Issue Resolution**:

   - How do you handle unexpected challenges or roadblocks that may arise during an implementation project?

   - Can you share a specific instance where you successfully resolved a significant issue during a project?

6. **References and Track Record**:

   - Could you provide references from past clients who have undergone Microsoft Dynamics 365 Business Central implementations with your assistance?

   - What notable achievements or successful outcomes have you had in recent implementations?

APPENDIX C

Project Scope Checklist

Using this checklist can help ensure that all aspects of the project's scope and deliverables are considered, documented, and agreed upon before moving forward with the implementation. This preparatory work is crucial for aligning expectations, setting the stage for a successful project, and avoiding potential challenges during the execution phase.

1. **Scope Statement:**

    - Craft a clear and concise scope statement.

    - Obtain approval from key stakeholders on the scope statement.

2. **Goals and Objectives:**

    - Identify and document the primary goals of the Business Central implementation.

    - Align Business Central objectives with overall business strategies.

© Dr. Gomathi S 2024
Dr. Gomathi S, *Mastering Microsoft Dynamics 365 Business Central,*
https://doi.org/10.1007/979-8-8688-0230-0

3. **Business Requirements:**

- Gather detailed business requirements from all relevant departments.

- Prioritize requirements based on business needs and impact.

4. **Technical Requirements:**

- Determine the technical specifications for Business Central customization.

- Outline integration needs with existing systems and data migration requirements.

5. **Project Deliverables:**

- Define specific deliverables, including software configurations, customizations, and reports.

- Ensure deliverables are measurable and quantifiable.

6. **Milestones:**

- Set major milestones for the project timeline.

- Link milestones to specific deliverables.

Plan for Phased Implementation:

- Determine if the Business Central implementation will be rolled out in phases.

- For each phase, define specific objectives, deliverables, and timelines.

- Ensure that each phase aligns with the overall project goals and objectives.

1. **Constraints:**

   - Document any constraints that may impact the project scope or timeline, such as budget limits or resource availability.

2. **Assumptions:**

   - List assumptions that are being made during planning, such as staff availability or technology capabilities.

3. **Exclusions:**

   - Clearly specify what is excluded from the project to avoid confusion and manage scope creep.

4. **Stakeholder Analysis:**

   - Identify all stakeholders and their influence/ interest in the project.

   - Document stakeholder requirements and expectations.

5. **Acceptance Criteria:**

   - Develop and document criteria for accepting completed deliverables.

   - Get stakeholder agreement on these criteria.

6. **Change Control Process:**

   - Establish a formal process for managing changes to the project scope.

   - Determine who has the authority to approve changes.

Deliverables Checklist

1. **Configuration and Setup:**

   - List all necessary configurations of Business Central modules.

   - Specify any required customizations to standard features.

2. **Data Migration:**

   - Outline the scope of data migration, including what data will be transferred.

   - Develop a data migration plan with clear deliverables.

3. **Integration:**

   - Identify third-party systems for integration with Business Central.

   - Describe the deliverables related to each integration point.

4. **User Training and Documentation:**

   - Define the extent of training materials and sessions to be provided.

   - Document the creation of user manuals and help guides.

5. **Testing:**

   - Determine the scope of testing, including phases like unit testing, system testing, and user acceptance testing.

   - Develop a testing plan with associated deliverables.

6. **Deployment:**

   - Outline the deployment plan, including phased rollouts or a single go-live event.

   - Clarify post-deployment support and maintenance deliverables.

7. **Reporting:**

   - Identify reporting needs and specify the delivery of custom report designs.

8. **Compliance and Security:**

   - Document compliance-related deliverables, if applicable.

   - Define security setup and measures within Business Central.

9. **Review and Approval:**

   - Schedule reviews for each deliverable with stakeholders.

   - Establish approval mechanisms for each deliverable.

10. **Post-implementation Review:**

    - Plan for a post-implementation review deliverable to assess project success and areas for improvement.

APPENDIX D

Functional Consultant's Checklist

Pre-migration:

1. **Understand Business Objectives:**

   - Align data migration objectives with business goals.

   - Engage stakeholders to define the scope and priorities of the migration.

2. **Data Analysis:**

   - Identify and categorize data sets for migration.

   - Review data quality and structure in current systems.

3. **Process Mapping:**

   - Map business processes to ensure that the new system supports all functionalities.

   - Define how each data type will be used in Business Central.

Dr. Gomathi S, *Mastering Microsoft Dynamics 365 Business Central*,
https://doi.org/10.1007/979-8-8688-0230-0

4. **Compliance and Regulation:**

- Ensure understanding of data protection laws relevant to the industry and regions.

- Define data privacy requirements for the migration.

Migration Planning:

1. **Data Migration Plan:**

- Develop a detailed data migration plan with timelines and milestones.

- Coordinate with the technical consultant to ensure technical feasibility.

2. **Data Cleansing:**

- Define data cleansing requirements.

- Supervise the data cleansing process to maintain data integrity.

3. **Customization and Integration Requirements:**

- Identify customization requirements and validate them once developed.

- Determine integration requirements, validate post-development, and confirm System Integration Testing (SIT).

4. **User Training and Documentation:**

- Plan for end-user training on the new system.

- Prepare user documentation and data dictionaries.

During Migration:

1. **Testing:**

   - Coordinate user acceptance testing (UAT) to ensure the new system meets business needs.

   - Verify data integrity and quality post-migration.

2. **Change Management:**

   - Manage the communication with business users regarding changes.

   - Address concerns and feedback from end users.

3. **User Permission Setup and Validation:**

   - Establish user permissions and validate their setup.

   - Role Center Configuration:

   - Configure role centers as per user roles and business needs.

Post-migration:

1. **Validation and Sign-Off:**

   - Validate that the migrated data meets all business requirements.

   - Obtain sign-off from business stakeholders.

2. **Support and Optimization:**

   - Provide post-migration support to users.

   - Optimize business processes based on new data insights.

3. **Go-Live Commencement:**

- Ensure readiness for the Go-Live phase.

- Prepare for immediate post Go-Live support to address any immediate issues or concerns.

APPENDIX E

Technical Consultant's Checklist

Pre-migration:

1. **Technical Assessment:**

   - Evaluate the existing technical infrastructure and requirements for Business Central.

   - Identify the tools and software required for migration.

2. **Data Preparation:**

   - Assist in data quality assessment from a technical standpoint.

   - Prepare data extraction procedures from legacy systems.

3. **Customization and Integration Planning:**

    - Develop customizations as per business requirements.

    - Plan and develop integrations with other systems.

    - Ensure security checks and validations are in place for customizations and integrations.

Migration Planning:

1. **Migration Tool Configuration:**

    - Set up and configure data migration tools.

    - Develop custom scripts or programs if necessary.

2. **Security Planning:**

    - Plan for data security during migration.

    - Implement encryption and secure transfer protocols.

3. **Backup and Recovery:**

    - Establish a comprehensive backup strategy for the migration.

    - Plan for recovery actions in case of migration failure.

During Migration:

1. **Execution of Migration:**

    - Perform data extraction, transformation, and loading (ETL) processes.

    - Monitor the migration process and troubleshoot issues as they arise.

2. **Data Verification:**

- Implement automated checks to verify data during migration.

- Collaborate with the functional consultant on data validation.

3. **System Integration Testing (SIT):**

- Conduct System Integration Testing for integrations and customizations.

- Address any issues identified during SIT.

Post-migration:

1. **System Testing:**

- Conduct system testing to ensure technical performance.

- Rectify any technical issues identified during testing.

2. **Documentation:**

- Document the technical details of the migration process.

- Update technical documentation based on the new system.

3. **Technical Support:**

- Provide technical support during the stabilization period.

- Assist in resolving post-migration technical issues.

4. **Go-Live Preparation:**

- Ensure readiness for the Go-Live phase.

- Prepare for immediate post Go-Live support, especially for customizations and integrations.

APPENDIX F

Technical Consultant's Go-Live Checklist

1. **System Performance Tuning:**

   - Confirm that performance tuning is complete.

   - Ensure the system is optimized for the expected load.

2. **Technical Infrastructure Validation:**

   - Verify that all hardware, client laptops, PCs, tablets, phones, barcode scanners, and infrastructure meet the requirements.

   - Check that network configurations support the Go-Live.

3. **Security and Compliance Checks:**

   - Ensure that security settings are enforced.

   - Verify compliance with relevant data protection and privacy laws.

© Dr. Gomathi S 2024
Dr. Gomathi S, *Mastering Microsoft Dynamics 365 Business Central*,
https://doi.org/10.1007/979-8-8688-0230-0

4. **Backup and Disaster Recovery:**

   - Test backup processes.

   - Validate that disaster recovery plans are in place and functional.

5. **System Integration Testing:**

   - Confirm that integrations with other systems are tested and operational.

   - Validate data flows between Business Central and integrated systems.

6. **Monitoring Tools Setup:**

   - Set up system monitoring tools for real-time insights.

   - Ensure alerting mechanisms are in place for system errors or performance issues.

7. **Final Technical Documentation:**

   - Ensure that all technical documentation is complete and up-to-date.

   - Document the system architecture, data models, and any custom development work.

8. **Cutover Execution:**

   - Execute technical tasks in the cutover plan, such as database migrations, system shutdowns, and start-ups.

   - Final Cutover Data Migration

   - Coordinate with the functional team on timing and sequence.

Index

A

Active Directory (AD), 9
ADKAR model, 176, 183–185, 193
Agile approach, 306
Agile methodology, 87
  ERP implementations, 91, 92
  hybrid strategy, ERP, 92
  implementation
     procedure, 89–91
  principles, 89
  requirements, 88
Artificial Intelligence (AI),
    311, 314, 324

B

Blockchain technology, 318
Bridges' transition model, 182, 185
Business Central
  application fields, 23–26
  cloud-based architecture, 1
  deployment, 30
  ERP system's, 29
  features, 1
    BI/reporting, 6
    customization/extension, 7, 8
    financial management, 3, 4

Microsoft 365, integration, 7
multi-language/multi-
  currency support, 10, 11
project cost management, 5, 6
sales and marketing, 5
scalability, 10
security and compliance, 8, 9
supply chain management, 4
functional consultant, 15–18
manufacturers, 27
Microsoft products, 2
retailers, 26, 27
service-based businesses, 28, 29
successful implementation,
  20, 22, 23
supplier management, 2
technical consultant, 12–14
Business Intelligence (BI), 6, 314, 324

C

California Consumer Privacy Act
  (CCPA), 139
Change management
  ADKAR model, 177–180
  challenges, 174–176
  methodology, 180–185

Printed in the United States
by Baker & Taylor Publisher Services